THE GROWTH MINDSET FOR TEEN GIRLS

SUCCESSFULLY TRANSFORM YOUR THINKING, BUILD CONFIDENCE, PROBLEM SOLVING SKILLS, AND INCREASE RESILIENCE IN JUST 30 DAYS

MARISA SUMMERS

CONTENTS

INTRODUCTION

Imagine finding a note on your desk that reads, "Warning: Your brain has been running on factory settings. Time to customize." That's essentially what discovering a growth mindset feels like. It's that moment when you realize everything you have believed about your abilities, intelligence, and potential is actually just Version 1.0 of yourself—and you're about to get the ultimate upgrade.

Relax—your current version is doing fine. It got you this far, after all. But like your favorite apps that don't stop evolving after launch, neither should you.

If you're familiar with how apps work, you'll know they rarely hit perfection at the onset. Developers are always refining and improving them with updates. That viral social media platform? It has changed so much you probably wouldn't recognize its early version. And guess what? Your brain works the same way—it needs regular "updates" to grow and adapt.

What makes this even more interesting is that *you're the developer* here. You decide how your brain evolves by what you take on and how you push yourself. Don't believe it? Try tackling that task you've been putting off. You'll not only get it done; it will also teach your brain how to stay calm and focused under pressure. Your every experience adds a new feature, and every challenge strengthens your mental performance. You're not stuck with where you are now; you're actually just getting started.

Yeah, I know—talking about growth is easy, but living it is a whole other deal. Life throws a lot at you—school, friends, family, and the never-ending social media pressures. They're a heavy load to carry, and all of it can consume your mind, making it harder for you to focus on progress. So, how are you supposed to think, *I can learn from this,* when anxiety and self-doubt keep telling you, *You'll fail* or *You're not good enough?* Add constant comparisons to the mix, and you'll likely see every step forward as a risk that's not worth taking.

Unfortunately, growth doesn't usually happen in your comfort zone. Avoiding challenges may feel safe in the moment, but it also locks you into your current limits.

Great, another adult telling me how to 'fix' myself. Thanks, but... Hold up —I need to stop that thinking of yours right there. This isn't about fixing you—because you're not broken. Not even close. This book is here to help you realize you're already whole and ready for the next chapter, not change who you are.

As a teenage girl, your brain is running on a sophisticated monthly biorhythm that affects everything from your energy levels to your problem-solving capabilities. You're also dealing with ancient biological processes—hormones, physical growth, and emotional development—while facing a world that's evolving at lightning speed. And when you think you're starting to get the hang of it, you're bombarded with mixed messages telling you who you should be, even as everyone insists you "be yourself." Sounds exhausting? That's because it is!

I see it in my daughter and her friends. They're all trying to solve this impossible equation—trying to make sense of their changing bodies, emotions, and rightful place in the world. They turn to social media influencers, online forums, and each other, hoping to find a formula that explains it all. But more often than not, instead of finding answers, they walk away feeling more confused than before.

And that's where mindset comes back into play. You see, the more they let themselves believe that confusion means something's wrong with them, the more they slip into a fixed mindset: *This is too hard* or *I'll never figure this out*. And when that happens, they get stuck in a cycle of frustration and avoidance.

That's why I decided to write this book. Not because I have all the answers—no one really does. I did because I understand both the science and the struggle. I've dedicated my career to breaking down complex systems into understandable parts and spent my life as a mother watching young women deal with the complexities of growing up in today's frenzied world.

We're living in an age where anyone can access the world's knowledge with a simple swipe of the fingers. You can learn calculus from YouTube, start businesses from your bedrooms, and connect with peers across the globe. Yet somehow, many of you constantly feel overwhelmed by the basic rhythms of daily life and your own bodies.

My children are perfect examples. They had so many deep questions about life and independence, but for the life of them, couldn't work out how to load the dishwasher and fold a fitted sheet properly. Laundry? Forget it—it was as if I had asked them to solve quantum physics. I quickly learned they needed detailed, step-by-step guidance for even the simplest tasks and that I had to remind myself every time not to take over and let them struggle through it—otherwise, they'd never learn.

Frankly speaking, these aren't failures of capability but of belief systems. Somewhere along the way, you girls have absorbed a set of instructions about what you can and can't do as well as who you should and shouldn't be. These invisible "algorithms" run quietly in the background of your lives, shaping your choices without you even realizing it.

Time to break free from those "algorithms!"

To be clear, however, this isn't going to be yet another book telling you how to be perfect. Think of it instead as your personal lab notebook for the greatest experiment you'll ever conduct: discovering who you really are and what you're capable of becoming. As a scientist, I know that understanding a system is the first step to optimizing it. And as a mother, I also know that more than just learning skills, growth involves helping our girls recognize the hidden beliefs and patterns that hold them back and giving them the tools to rewrite those scripts. This book can help you do exactly that.

Over the next eight chapters, we'll take a closer look at growth mindset from every angle. You'll learn how it feels in real life, how it changes your perspective, and how it can redefine your relationship with challenges.

Along the way, we'll also explore the actual science behind why you feel the way you do, decode your energy and emotion patterns, and develop practical strategies for working with your natural rhythms. Most importantly, we'll do it all while honoring the incredible complexity of who you are.

By the time you finish this book, you'll have the skills to debug toxic thought patterns, upgrade your self-talk, and install new confidence "protocols" that don't depend on the number of likes and followers and other external sources of validation.

Adulting was simpler for your moms—they had slower lives, clearer rules, and no distracting smartphones buzzing every 10 seconds.

You, though, are pioneering what it means to grow up in the digital age. No manual exists for this. But who cares? Your brain is in its prime, wired to learn at breakneck speed, adapt to new challenges, and shape the world around you. So, take control and build the life you want!

1

GROWTH MINDSET TAILORED TO TEEN GIRLS

We learn a lot in school: algebra, ancient history, and how our DNA basically makes us who we are (shoutout to genetics class!). Yet somehow, one of the most important topics—the way our bodies function—doesn't get much attention.

Maybe you've sat through an awkward health class or two, but they usually skip the good stuff, including the fact that your body is running on an extremely sophisticated schedule. No, seriously. It's real science, not some made-up horoscope nonsense!

More interestingly, this cycle is an essential factor in determining your focus, energy levels, and mood throughout the month. This means you'll go from *I'm a genius!* to *Why can't I even function?* depending on the phase you're in. The problem is that most girls have no clue it's happening. Instead, they're pressured to perform at full speed 24/7, with hardly any room for much-needed rest. Needless to say, that's a one-way ticket to burnout city.

Which brings us to this chapter. You're about to learn something that most people—adults included—never get the chance to fully understand: how to recognize the body's patterns and use them to your advantage. Together, we'll look into the secret rhythm that impacts everything, from your energy levels to your social skills; from your creative bursts to your problem-solving abilities. No more fighting against your cycle—it's time you work with it and unleash your full potential.

GIRLS' 30-DAY HORMONAL CYCLE EXPERIENCE VS. BOYS' 24-HOUR HORMONAL RHYTHM

Girls and guys tend to run on slightly different internal clocks. His body operates on a simple 24-hour schedule, with his main hormone, testosterone, following a daily rhythm that repeats similar to clockwork.

Testosterone levels peak in the morning, giving him a surge of energy, confidence, and focus. That's why most guys feel ready to conquer the world first thing in the morning. By early afternoon, though, testosterone dips, and with it comes the infamous afternoon slump—suddenly, he's zoning out and looking for snacks instead of staying productive. At night, testosterone levels hit their lowest, which helps them wind down and relax. Perfect timing for Netflix, gaming, or crashing early.

The next day? Same story, same cycle. This daily repetition actually works in their favor. Without sudden hormonal shifts derailing their energy or focus, they can maintain a stable pace, track their progress, and build momentum. It's a solid foundation for forming habits and staying on top of goals (Brambilla et al., 2009).

Your body, on the flip side, is a bit more elaborate. Sure, you've got that same 24-hour clock ticking away. But beneath that, you're also running a 30-day masterpiece of biological engineering. (*In fact, the*

30-day mark isn't a universal truth for every gal out there. The normal cycle for teenage girls normally lasts anywhere from around 21 to 38 days. Some might even have cycles that color outside those lines, with shorter or longer durations, particularly when they're period freshmen.)

Just as the moon cycles between its phases, from new to full and back again, your body moves through a cosmic cycle with *four* distinct stages. Right now, as you're reading this, a microscopic revolution's happening somewhere in your body. Hormones are hard at work, fluctuating in levels like an ever-changing tide. These hormonal shifts trigger all kinds of internal changes so subtly that your mood and attention can swing from one minute to the next without you even realizing why (Fletcher, 2019).

In a little while, we'll break down how this cycle works and affects you physically and emotionally as the weeks go by. Why does this matter? Because understanding this rhythm gives you the "cheat codes" to take better control of your life. Those days when you're bursting with energy—raring to write a novel, solve world hunger, and nail that TikTok dance trend all before lunch?—there's a reason for that. The times when you'd rather build a blanket fort and hide from humanity? That's part of the process too. Once you start recognizing it, you can learn to work with your body rather than constantly resisting it.

But that's a topic for the next section. For now, I just need you to trust the process—your body knows exactly what it's doing. It has a master plan, working seamlessly behind the scenes, even when it doesn't feel that way. If you don't recognize this, these natural fluctuations might throw you off balance. You could end up pushing yourself too hard during low-energy phases or blaming yourself for not being "good enough" when, in reality, it's just a temporary shift in your cycle.

To stay motivated and confident, you need to work with these natural fluctuations. Growth mindset strategies prove effective when they match your body's rhythm. Awareness is your key to making this work.

Remember, you're not moody; you're cyclical. You're not inconsistent; you're adaptable. While the boys are running on a simple stopwatch, you're operating an astronomical clock. Own it. Rock it. Use it to your advantage.

IMPACT OF HORMONAL CHANGES ON GROWTH MINDSET

Every second of every day, your body manages a flow of hormones that not only drive physical changes but rewire your brain and influence your mindset as well. This ongoing renovation is essential for growth; however, it also causes temporary instability in how you process information and handle challenges.

And that's why mastering your mindset isn't simply a matter of willpower and positive thinking. Of course, those things still play a huge role, but they're most effective when you understand and respect your body's natural cycle. At the end of the day, forcing yourself to stay at 100% all the time is neither practical nor sustainable, especially when it conflicts with your brain's natural rhythms.

Mood Swings, Fatigue, and Reduced Confidence

You've probably had those days where you wake up and feel like the queen of the universe. You're unstoppable. Homework? Done. Friends? Happy. Life? Perfect. And then... BOOM. By lunch, you somehow transform into a blob of sadness and self-doubt, where fumbling to open a water bottle leaves you wondering whatever happened to your superhero powers.

What's going on? The answer lies in your body's hormonal mix—specifically, the big three: estrogen, progesterone, and testosterone. These guys are in charge of a lot during puberty: growth spurts, body development, and yes, your moods. And that can take a toll on your mindset.

Fun Fact #1:

Testosterone isn't exclusive to boys. Girls have it too, though in smaller amounts! It helps with stuff like boosting energy, building muscle, and keeping your mood in check. Who knew hormones could be so multi-talented?

To be more specific, when your hormones fluctuate, they affect your brain's key areas, including the amygdala (which processes emotions) and the prefrontal cortex (which handles rational thinking and decision-making).

During these shifts, the amygdala can become more reactive, making you more prone to stress and negative thoughts. At the same time, the prefrontal cortex—your brain's logic center—may not function as smoothly, causing clear thinking and perspective to slip away. This combination can make you jump to extreme conclusions, like, *I'll never be good at math*, instead of the more balanced thought, *This is hard now, but I can improve.*

When you're tired, frustrated, or overwhelmed, these brain processes struggle even more. Your mind leans heavily on the negative, which can trap you in a *fixed mindset*—the belief that your abilities are static and can't improve.

These fluctuations, however, are completely normal, as they're signs that your brain is developing in exactly the way it should. In other words, having days when you feel less confident or motivated doesn't erase your abilities. You're not suddenly less capable because you FEEL less so. Think of it this way: If you're an awesome basketball player, you don't lose those skills because you're having an off day. The skills are still there; they're just temporarily harder to access (Ali et al., 2018).

But why do your hormones keep playing this unsteady game of highs and lows? Well, they aren't acting randomly. Your body operates on a well-structured hormonal cycle designed to support growth, development, and reproductive health. You may need to head to the next section to learn what's really happening.

Hormonal Shifts Throughout the Cycle

Hormones love a good cycle—especially the ones running the show in your body. Each month, estrogen, progesterone, and testosterone move through a set routine, with predictable peaks and dips, if you pay close attention to the signals your body is sending.

Phase 1: The Follicular Phase

From the first day of your period to ovulation, you're in the follicular phase where estrogen steadily rises, enhancing your mental clarity and physical energy.

As estrogen increases, you may feel more focused, energized, and motivated. Confidence may then follow, along with a sense of optimism and readiness to tackle challenges head-on.

However, this surge in energy doesn't happen right away. At the start of your period, you might still feel fatigued and drained due to physical factors such as cramps, bloating, and blood loss.

Phase 2: Ovulation

Ovulation hits right in the middle of your cycle when you're at your best. Estrogen peaks, giving you a mental edge. You become more confident, your social skills are on point, and solving tough problems seems way easier than usual.

This is also the time when testosterone briefly spikes, offering you an extra push in motivation, competitiveness, and drive. Just a heads-up: This surge is temporary; after ovulation, hormone levels start shifting in a new direction. So, enjoy it while it lasts!

Fun Fact #2:

Progesterone subtly increases your body temperature after ovulation. It's a small shift, but during the luteal phase, you may feel the warmth creeping in. This is totally a natural part of your cycle—your body's just preparing for what's to come next!

Phase 3: The Luteal Phase

Progesterone is the main player at this stage. It encourages rest and recovery, promoting better sleep and calming your nervous system, which is great for balance. That said, it can also sap your energy and motivation. The body's shift to this "low-power mode" means you have less energy available for activities that require stamina and drive. You might notice that your focus isn't as sharp, and you find tasks that were manageable a week ago harder to complete now.

Furthermore, your mood may remain stable for a while, but as you move further into the luteal phase, both estrogen and progesterone start to drop. This hormonal dip affects serotonin production (aka your brain's "feel-good" chemical that helps keep your mood balanced and happy).

With less serotonin, everyday stress hits harder, irritations pile up more quickly, and your mind may lean toward negativity. You know those moments when a random remark hits harder than it should and tears start to build? Yep, you can blame lower serotonin levels for that.

Phase 4: Premenstrual Days

Hormones hit rock bottom here, particularly estrogen and serotonin, which can throw everything out of whack.

Physically, your muscles may feel heavier and tire out way faster than usual. That's because your body is prepping for menstruation, which can mess with your energy reserves and stamina. The estrogen decline likewise heightens emotional sensitivity. As a result, you may get irritable and anxious more easily or feel completely drained. To make things tougher, you may find it harder to stay engaged and zone out more frequently.

Nonetheless, this is just the point in your cycle where your brain and body are "begging" you to slow down and recharge. And if you ask me, this isn't a sign of weakness—it's a natural drop in energy that your body is designed to handle (Goyanka et al., 2024).

__Fun Fact #3:__

Progesterone doesn't just say, "Rest up!" It's also quietly writing your dreams. Higher levels during the luteal phase can lead to more vivid dreams. So, if you're suddenly dreaming about your crush in a bizarre rom-com, you can thank progesterone for that late-night fantasy production!

Your hormonal cycle is part of an intricate biological system that has evolved over millions of years. Each phase brings its own characteristic. Nature literally gives you the ability to access different cognitive and physical strengths at different times. That's not an inconvenience—that's a superpower. So, don't ever fall into the trap of looking at these natural rhythms as limitations. Would you expect to be able to sprint at top speed indefinitely? I bet you wouldn't. Your hormonal cycle works similarly; it's meant to include both periods of high performance and necessary recovery.

Key Takeaways:

• Your body's on a 30-day cycle, not just a 24-hour one.

• Hormones = brain influencers.

• Four phases, four moods.

• Work with your cycle: Know when to push and when to chill.

2

IMPOSTER SYNDROME AND LIMITATIONS

I've been thinking a lot about why we're so hard on ourselves. I used to have no clue—I just thought it was weird how our best moments can also be when our brain works hardest against us. Like, who invited that voice to the party? You know that feeling when you crush a test—I mean really nail it—but there's this little voice whispering, *You just happened to get lucky.* Or when you give that amazing presentation, but instead of celebrating, you obsess over that one tiny *um* in the middle?

The crazier part? The better you are at something, the more likely you are to doubt yourself. And if you're nodding along right now, you're probably the kind of person I'm talking about—someone who's really capable but can't quite believe it. And get this—some of the most talented people feel the same way.

Dr. Maya Angelou (yes, the famous writer) once said she felt like a fraud every time she published a new book—and she wrote 11 of them (Ma, 2017)! She candidly shared, "I have written 11 books, but each time I think, *Uh oh, they're going to find out now. I've run a game on everybody, and they're going to find me out.'* Even Michelle Obama has openly discussed her feelings of self-doubt, admitting, "I still have a little imposter syndrome. It never goes away, that you're actually listening to me." Wait, Michelle Obama? The woman who's inspired millions and ran the White House with utmost grace? That's like Beyoncé wondering if she's ever good at performing. Wild, but it happens (Leadem, 2017)!

The good news is that this isn't some kind of personal curse or flaw. Turns out, it's so common that researchers even gave it a name: imposter syndrome—and for many girls, it's an unwelcome companion on their road to success.

IMPOSTER SYNDROME: WHEN SUCCESS FEELS FAKE

Welcome to what psychologists call imposter syndrome. Sounds fancy, right? But really, it's a scientific term for that feeling of being a fraud even when you're clearly aren't. And I'll admit, I was surprised to learn that this whole thing was first discovered because of some seriously smart women.

In 1978, two psychologists, Dr. Pauline Rose Clance and Dr. Suzanne Imes, noticed something odd. They were studying some super successful women—we're talking top-of-their-class, crushing-it-at-work kind of women—and found out that tons of them secretly believed they were not good enough. These women were convinced they had somehow "tricked" everyone into thinking they were smart. Despite their accomplishments, they feared being "exposed" as unintelligent or incapable.

Over time, this feeling became known as imposter syndrome, and it's now recognized as a widespread issue affecting people of all genders, though research suggests it disproportionately affects girls and women (Clance & Imes, 1978).

Imagine you have this awesome Instagram filter that makes everything look slightly wrong. Not obviously so—just enough to make you question what you're seeing. Maybe the lighting is off or the colors look strange, but you can't quite put your finger on what's wrong. That's what imposter syndrome does to your view of yourself. You accomplish something cool, but this mental filter immediately jumps in and says, "*Yeah, but...*"

Of course, imposter syndrome is not mainly about getting bad vibes. It gets in your way, making things way harder to do the following:

- **Own your wins:** Imposter syndrome stops you from giving yourself credit. And when you don't take time to recognize your successes, your brain struggles to learn from them. You put away your trophies in a case, never bothering to put them on display. Without that recognition, you can't grow because you lose sight of how far you've come.
- **Keep growing:** Constant self-doubt makes it difficult to focus on improving. Thoughts like *How can I get better?* are drowned out by *What if I'm not good enough?* So, it's pretty clear why girls who experience strong imposter syndrome would avoid stepping outside their comfort zones, not because they can't handle it, but because they're scared of confirming their fears.
- **Reframe feedback:** Self-doubt can twist the meaning of feedback, turning helpful advice into a harsh critique in your mind. Rather than seeing it as a guide to help you improve, you might fixate on the negative comments, believing that they reflect your entire worth. This reaction then prevents you from recognizing areas for growth and using feedback as a learning opportunity.
- **Be confident in yourself:** Imposter syndrome messes with your confidence, making you doubt your every choice. You start putting too much weight on what others think instead of relying on your own judgment and skills.

- **Maintain resilience:** One mistake and imposter syndrome has you thinking it's over for you. Before you know it, your mind's in overdrive. Thoughts race—every little detail you could've done better haunts you. You beat yourself up until you feel too stuck to try again, a sure way to lose your resilience and get trapped in self-doubt.

Back to that whole gender thing, you might wonder why we girls seem to get hit with imposter syndrome more than the boys. And no, it's not because we're born with an extra dose of self-doubt! It's more because of the messages we absorb from the world around us.

Do you know how your phone picks up nearby Wi-Fi signals? Well, we're constantly picking up signals ourselves from movies, social media, and even casual comments. When you rarely see someone who's like you doing the thing you want to do, or when people seem surprised by your success ("Wow, you're really good at math... for a girl!"), your brain starts playing an annoying game of *Maybe I don't really belong here*. These mental messages build up layer by layer, making that imposter feeling heavier for us than it needs to be.

Simply put, you aren't naturally more prone to self-doubt; it's that we're living in a world that's continues to adjust its expectations. Every time we see a male-dominated field or hear about roles portrayed as "not for girls," our brains file that away, even when the logical part of you knows better.

But how exactly do these societal pressures work? How do they make us question ourselves despite clear evidence of our abilities?

Next up, we'll go deeper into how gender stereotypes reinforce imposter syndrome.

Once you understand how these stereotypes operate, you can break free from their grip. And when you see them for what they are, you can't unsee them—better yet, you can start to question them. Why shouldn't a girl dream of being both a scientist and an athlete? Why can't she code video games and lead a tech company? The answer is: She definitely can. But first, we need to recognize and challenge these limiting beliefs that have been quietly shaping our choices all along.

Reality Check: Do You Actually Have Imposter Syndrome? Let's Find Out.

Before you label yourself an imposter, answer these questions:

- **Have you scammed your way into success using magic, bribery, or secret hypnosis techniques? (No, charming your way through a group project doesn't count here.)**

- **Have you hacked into the system to give yourself fake credentials?**

- **Are you secretly three raccoons in a trench coat pretending to be human?**

If you answered "no" to all of the above, Congrats! You're NOT an imposter. Just a perfectly capable human who sometimes doubts themselves (which is normal).

GENDER STEREOTYPES AND THEIR LASTING IMPACT

In a toy store, have you ever seen how the toys are separated by gender, with "boys" on one side and "girls" on the other?

The "girls" side explodes with pink princess stuff and dolls, while the "boys" side is stocked with science kits, building blocks, and sports equipment. Seems pretty harmless, doesn't it? Nope. These small, everyday patterns, unfortunately, contribute to something bigger:

stereotypes that can totally mess with how we see ourselves. They stand as invisible walls—you can't see them, but somehow they're still in your way.

I know a girl named Lily, who loved taking apart her family's old electronics to figure out how they worked. But when she told her parents she wanted to be an engineer, they looked at her funny, saying, "Isn't that more of a guy thing?" Even though she excels in math and science, those words kept echoing in her head more and more each day. Eventually, she chose a different career, not because she lost interest in the field but simply because her parents' words made her believe she didn't belong in it.

According to research conducted by Lin Bian, Sarah-Jane Leslie, and Andrei Cimpian, published in the journal Science in 2017, girls as young as six begin believing that certain activities or careers are "not for them" based solely on gender stereotypes (Bian, Leslie, & Cimpian, 2017). Six! That's even before most of us lost our baby teeth!

The same thing happens with leadership roles. A 2018 article in The New York Times and a report from Warwick Business School noted that when people are asked to draw a leader, the majority—regardless of gender—tend to depict a man (Kiefer, 2018; Murphy, 2018).

Women can absolutely lead—no question about that. That said, we've been surrounded by so many images of male leaders that our brains start to automatically make that connection. Eleanor Roosevelt (activist and former U.S. First Lady), Harriet Tubman (abolitionist and Underground Railroad leader), and Queen Victoria (monarch who shaped an entire era) were among history's greatest leaders. Still, they don't get the same enduring recognition as the male figures like Winston Churchill, Julius Caesar, and Abraham Lincoln. What's up with that?

Sports are yet another battleground for stereotypes. Despite the fact that women's sports have given us some of the most incredible moments in athletic history, girls still receive comments like "Don't get too muscular" or "That sport isn't feminine." The Women's Sports Foundation reports that by age 14, girls drop out of sports at twice the rate of boys. This gap is fueled by a combination of social stigma and the outdated belief that sports are in some way "less appropriate" for girls (*Do You Know the Factors Influencing Girls' Participation in Sports?*, n.d.).

Fun Fact #4:

Before Title IX (a law that said schools had to give girls equal sports opportunities), people literally thought girls were too "delicate" for competitive sports. Athletics programs for girls barely existed—and if they did, they received minimal funding, if any at all.

Dr. Carol Dweck, who's the Sherlock Holmes of studying how our minds work, found that these stereotypes do something even sneakier: They can trick us into developing what we already know—a "fixed mindset." Her research also revealed that many extremely talented girls were the ones most likely to fall into this trap. That's because they'd often been praised their whole lives for being "naturally smart" or "gifted." So when they hit challenges (which everyone does eventually), they freaked out (Dweck, 2008).

The truth is, every field thrives on diversity—whether it's STEM, leadership, or sports. What happens if every song on your playlist sounds exactly the same? Or the most-followed TikTok creators come up with identical content? Boring, right? That's essentially what happens when we let stereotypes push girls away from certain fields. Different perspectives lead to creative breakthroughs, fresh solutions, and success stories that can change the game for everyone. If girls step back because of outdated stereotypes, everyone loses.

Think I'm overstating it? Check out these real-life examples:

In the early development of automotive safety features, such as airbags, design and testing were predominantly conducted by all-male teams using crash test dummies modeled after average-sized men. This male-centric approach led to safety measures that did not adequately account for women and children. Consequently, when airbags deployed, the force was too strong for smaller occupants, resulting in increased risk of injury and fatalities among women and children. Between 1996 and 2000, there were 179 deaths attributed to this issue (Frye, Ko, Kotnik, & Zelt, 2021). Yikes!

Or how about this mind-bender: Artificial intelligence is learning to be biased. No joke. When AI is trained mainly by one group of people (guess who?), it starts showing some serious prejudices. Just look at early facial recognition software—it couldn't accurately identify women of color because—surprise!—the teams creating it didn't include many women of color. The outcome? A technology that failed many of the people it was supposed to serve.

Fun Fact #5:

Once upon a time, computer programming was a women-dominated field. Yep, it was seen as routine and administrative, so women were the go-to coders. But when it got viewed as prestigious and profitable, out of nowhere, it became a "man's profession."

Did you know that we don't have as much information about heart attacks in women as we do in men? For years, medical research mainly focused on male subjects. Hence, doctors sometimes miss heart attacks in women since they're looking for "classic" symptoms —which turn out to be classic male symptoms. Women often have completely different warning signs, and we're still catching up on this knowledge (Hardesty, 2018).

This makes it more certain that the biggest challenges that our world faces—climate change, healthcare access, and social inequality— need all hands on deck. Most importantly, the world doesn't need more of the same. It needs more diverse dreamers, problem-solvers, and powerful leaders. It's wanting of girls stepping up and owning their space in fields where they've been underrepresented for far too long. It needs you. This isn't solely a matter of fairness; it's a necessity for improving innovation and safety on a global scale.

How many times have you had a great idea but didn't have the guts to raise your hand? Or avoided joining a club because you thought you wouldn't fit in? That, right there, is how innovation and creativity get stifled—one self-doubt at a time. Your perspective, your ideas, your way of thinking—they're like your fingerprints. Nobody else has exactly the same ones. And that's what makes your voice so valuable. Without it, the world misses out on what only you can offer.

Don't let self-doubt be the reason you stay silent. Don't allow your fear of judgment stop you from stepping up. The greatest ideas, the boldest changes, and the most inspiring movements all started with someone who simply dared to speak, even when they weren't sure how their words would be received. After all, confidence isn't about never doubting yourself but not letting doubt make your decisions for you.

Pro Tip:

I like to think of imposter syndrome as an overprotective friend in my head—one that tries to keep me safe by

**keeping my expectations low. It means well, but some-
times, it needs a gentle reminder that I'm stronger than it
thinks I am. Maybe you should remind yours too.**

And perhaps you won't believe what I'm about to say, but these feelings of self-doubt actually peak in people who push themselves to
grow (Godwin, 2025). In other words, feeling like an imposter often
means you're doing something right—you're challenging yourself
and stepping out of your comfort zone. However, it also feels as if
growth and self-doubt are travel companions—where one goes, the
other follows. Yes, it may be uncomfortable, but if you choose to step
forward anyway, you'll come out stronger. Weirdly enough, people
with actual imposter syndrome tend to be the ones who work the
hardest, care the most, and genuinely deserve to be where they are.
The real imposters don't worry about being imposters.

This also implies that we're not here to eliminate your self-doubt
entirely. That's about as realistic as never feeling hungry. Our goal
here is to understand why those doubts pop up and what they really
mean. Athletes learn how to tell the difference between discomfort
that signals progress and pain that indicates harm. Similarly, you can
learn to distinguish between productive doubt, which helps you
grow, and destructive doubts, which can only hold you back.

Perpetually freaking out about exams? If you've put in the work,
relax, and say farewell to those worries—you don't need them! If a
last-minute doubt reminded you of a forgotten chapter, just consider
it a blessing. You've got one more chance to review! Observe your
doubt, simply recognize it for what it is, and you'll find things
become much easier.

Key Takeaways:

• Imposter syndrome isn't proof that you're unqualified.

• Stereotypes shape confidence more than we realize.

• The more talented you are, the more your brain might trick you into thinking you're not.

• Not all doubts are bad: Some uncertainties push you to improve, while other kinds just hold you back. Learn to tell the difference.

• If you're worried about being a fraud, that's proof you're not one.

• Second-guessing yourself is a side effect of growth. Keep pushing forward nonetheless.

3
FEAR OF FAILURE

Everyone's afraid of something.

Even your favorite pop star, Ariana Grande, who performs in front of thousands, has opened up about her struggles with anxiety (*14 celebrities who've openly discussed their anxiety struggles,* n.d.). Even your mom, who somehow always knows what to do, has nights where fear keeps her wide awake. So, if you're scared of failure, cool. You're exactly where you should be. No shame in it. No need to hide.

Scientifically, your brain is wired to see failure as a threat, and it reacts by going into full-on freakout mode. But before you start blaming evolution for your sweaty palms, let's unpack why this fear exists—and more crucially, how you can make peace with it.

HOW YOUR BRAIN OVERREACTS TO FEAR

Fear isn't bad; it's actually essential. Without it, who knows? You could be that person leaping between rooftops in a parkour attempt gone wrong. It's your internal safety system, slamming the brakes in time to avoid disaster. Annoying, yes—especially when you just want some peace from the non-stop internal alarm.

Long ago—like, caveman days—our ancestors needed fear to survive. Imagine yourself in that period—you're out hunting for berries and you suddenly hear a rustle behind you. Fear kicks in. Your heart races, your senses sharpen, and your body prepares to fight or run faster than Usain Bolt. Had fear not existed, our ancient ancestors might have thought it was a good idea to pet saber-toothed tigers or befriend grizzly bears. Fear kept them alive long enough to eventually become us. Fear is literally programmed into our DNA as a survival superpower.

Fast forward to today; you're not dodging ferocious animals anymore, but your brain doesn't know that. It still treats anything scary, such as social embarrassment or rejection, as a threat. Failure? It's filed under "major threat" in your mental database, right next to spiders and public speaking.

Truth be told, your brain doesn't really care whether you're facing an actual tiger or just the possibility of messing up your class presentation. To your nervous system, threat is threat. When your fear of failure creeps up, the amygdala flips out. This little almond-shaped drama queen controls your fear response, and it can't tell the difference between a failed math test and an actual emergency.

Your body gets ready for battle, with the heart beating faster to pump more blood to your muscles. Your breathing quickens to get more oxygen. Your pupils dilate to see better. Your palms might get sweaty (which actually helped our ancestors grip tree branches better when escaping predators—how cool is that?). Meanwhile, your rational brain (the prefrontal cortex) mutters, *Chill, it's not that deep*, but it struggles to be heard over the noise (Marsh, 2024).

During adolescence, the amygdala and prefrontal cortex are still developing, and hormonal shifts make teens more emotionally reactive. Their brains amplify fear responses, particularly when under stress. Cortisol, the primary stress hormone, plays a bigger role here, making their "fight or flight" response stronger (Romeo, 2013; Blakemore, 2019). Factor in the constant social media pressures, where every mistake could become tomorrow's viral embarrassment, and you've got a perfect storm of failure fear.

THE WALLS THAT BLOCK YOUR DREAMS

Failure. That word hit a nerve, didn't it? It's a word so heavy it can make your stomach sink faster than a canceled Netflix season finale. It's not the failure itself that trips us up—it's the fear of it. Sometimes the fear of messing up pushes you toward perfectionism. Other times, it's the fear of being judged that keeps you from sharing your ideas. Or maybe it's the fear of disappointing others, locking you into constant people-pleasing. Each one has its own way of holding you back, but they all work toward the same goal: to keeping you stuck.

Fear of Making Mistakes: The Trap of Perfectionism

Some people get stuck fearing committing even the smallest mistakes, thinking they're red flags for failure. This can bring on waves of shame, self-doubt, and that oh-so-fun fear of being judged by others. To cope, they shrink from risks and new challenges at all costs. For girls, the fear of making mistakes, also known as *mistake-avoidance anxiety*, is usually tied to perfectionism, a weighty burden shaped by society's quiet demand to always be perfect.

Dr. Brené Brown, a research professor at the University of Houston, who's spent years studying perfectionism, found something fascinating: that the people most trapped by perfectionism aren't actually the ones striving for excellence; they're those who are most afraid of shame.

She describes perfectionism as "a self-destructive and addictive belief system that fuels this primary thought: *If I look perfect and do everything perfectly, I can avoid or minimize the painful feelings of blame, judgment, and shame.*" That straight-A student who won't join the debate team? The talented artist who never shares her work? They're not lacking abilities—they're caught in what many refer to as the "perfectionism paralysis"—a state where fear of imperfection prevents action and growth (Brown, 2010).

Furthermore, while boys are often praised and encouraged to take risks and show courage, girls would receive different messages—to be careful, proper, and perfect. This can create increased pressure on them to avoid mistakes in order to maintain a "perfect" image. These expectations result in what psychologists and sociologists call a "double bind"—conflicting demands where a person is placed in a no-win situation. No matter which choice they make, they face criticism or failure (Damour, 2019; Bateson et al., 1956). For example, girls are expected to:

- be highly successful but not appear overly ambitious.
- be attractive but not vain.
- achieve perfection but never show struggle.

Simply put, if you try too hard, you may be labeled as overly ambitious or intense; if you underperform, you can get criticized for not meeting high standards.

The biggest downside of perfectionism isn't the doors it closes; it's the way it makes failure feel even more unbearable. Continually avoiding potential mistakes can make you more emotionally reactive to failure, not less (Nelson et al., 2018). And you know what? Life becomes surprisingly small when you need a guarantee before trying anything new. You won't step forward unless you're 100% sure you'd nail it. So, you stick to the rooms you know, paths you've walked before, and choices that feel safe. No surprises, no mistakes, no disappointments—but also no discoveries.

In the end, what would you discover if you gave yourself permission to fail—and learn from it? Isn't the risk of missing out on growth far greater than the fear of getting it wrong?

Fun Fact #6:

It took Thomas Edison over 1,000 failed attempts to get the lightbulb right (Hendry, 2013). Lucky for us, he wasn't a quitter... or our best source of light would still be a campfire and a strong prayer.

Fear of Rejection and Criticism: The Approval-Seeking Loop

Raise your hand if you've ever stopped yourself from doing something because you were afraid someone might laugh or judge you. Again, this fear of rejection or criticism isn't just some thing your brain made up one day to mess with you. It's hardwired into us as humans.

Humans are social creatures, and for most of human history, being accepted by your group was a matter of survival. Thousands of years ago, if you messed up and got kicked out of the tribe, it wasn't like you could Uber to the next village. Isolation meant danger, and in the worst-case scenario, you'd wind up as dinner for some hungry prehistoric predator. Safety came from belonging, and that instinct to avoid rejection stuck with us. Evolution really did us dirty on this one.

Now, in modern life, that same ancient system is still in overdrive. Your brain might process that presentation in class as dangerous as facing down a jungle carnivore. Those butterflies in your stomach before sharing an idea? That's your ancient survival system screaming "DANGER!" even though the worst that could happen is someone saying "nah."

Social media has only made things worse. The pressure doesn't stop with the twenty-something people in your class; you're open to judgment from hundreds or even thousands of people online. Each post becomes a mini-referendum on your worthiness. A curious observation is that teens who are more sensitive to rejection tend to use social media differently. They frequently obsess over likes and comments or carefully curate their online presence to avoid any possibility of criticism.

Have you ever felt like your true personality is slowly getting lost in the quest for validation? Has fear of criticism ever stopped you from celebrating your own wins? Do you often second-guess what you post because you're worried people might misinterpret it? Be real with yourself. It's the only way to build authentic relationships where you feel truly seen and accepted. If you don't, low self-worth can trap you in a self-fulfilling prophecy—your fears keep you distant from others, preventing meaningful connections and rein- forcing the belief that you're misunderstood (Lopez & Rice, 2006).

J.K. Rowling's Harry Potter was rejected by 12 publishers (Millington, 2018). Lady Gaga was dropped by her first record label (Beaudoin, 2015). Even Taylor Swift got turned down by countless Nashville record labels before getting her big break (Willman, 2008). Rejection didn't stop them—it pushed them. It can push you too.

Let's change how you think about rejection. Be brave enough to face it, but don't let it become your identity. Every time someone doesn't love your idea, see it as information—feedback that helps you learn, adapt, and grow.

The Fear of Disappointing Others: Why We All Live Up to Everyone Else's Standards

The fear of disappointing others boils down to one simple thing: expectations. Feeling that failure isn't yours alone—that it also affects parents, friends, teachers, and everyone who believes in you —is common.

Excellent grades, flawless appearance, enviable social life. And don't forget the perfect social media feed—when it's not all in place, guilt and shame could set in when you care so much about others' opinions, even if you know you shouldn't.

Similar to other fears, this one isn't purely an emotional response— it has deep biological roots. The brain processes the fear of disappointing loved ones the same way the fear of physical pain does. In simpler terms, the weight of disappointing someone can hit you with the force of a gut punch. This is the brain's way of signaling that something is wrong in your social relationships. You want to avoid it because humans are naturally wired to seek social approval.

This fear can quickly spiral out of control if not managed. When you become too absorbed in avoiding disappointment or always trying to please others, it starts to chip away at your own sense of self. You may begin to ignore your own desires and needs to meet other people's expectations. You tie your self-worth to external validation, and that's a dangerous place to be.

Keep in mind that you are not responsible for other people's emotions. Sure, caring about the feelings of those you love matters, but the ones who truly care about you don't demand perfection. They need you to be genuine and give your best effort—and that's all they expect.

Not to mention, you can't please everyone, especially when different people come with varied expectations and they start contradicting each other. I mean, how are you supposed to balance everything when your parents want you to fulfill their dreams, your friends need you to hang out with and be there for them, and your extracurriculars require extra time and effort?

There's a world of difference between falling short of others' hopes and labeling yourself a failure. Disappointing someone doesn't necessarily make you disappointing. Read that again! Real growth happens when you make decisions that align with your values, not with your fears.

OVERCOMING THE FEAR OF FAILURE

The belief that failure reflects a personal inadequacy is where the real problem begins. Instead of viewing challenges as opportunities for growth, you see them as evidence that you aren't capable or worthy. And this is one of the most limiting mindsets you can have.

Is there anyone on this planet who has never failed? Not one single person. If they tell you otherwise, they're lying—or they've lived the most boring, risk-free life imaginable, which honestly sounds even worse than failing.

Trust me, you failed before you even knew what failure was. The first time you tried to walk? Boom—face-first into the carpet. Learning to ride a bike? Probably ended with scraped knees and a dramatic vow to never go near a bike again. Remember trying to write your name in kindergarten? That "A" looked like it had been through a tornado. Interestingly, you didn't sit there and think, *Well, I guess walking just isn't for me.* You kept wobbling, pedaling, and scribbling until you finally figured out how to do them properly.

So, why now—when you're older, stronger, and smarter—does failing suddenly seem so terrifying? Fear only stings when you're certain it has teeth.

Enough of the old script—time to take back your power. Let's go!

Normalizing Struggle and Failure

Society loves to celebrate success, but it conveniently skips over the messy parts that led there. You see the highlight reels—gold medals, perfect grades, award-winning performances—but not the late-night studying, the rejections, the falling flat on your face (sometimes literally). And that's the problem. We grow up thinking struggle is not the way to go when it's actually the most normal thing ever.

Thankfully, adopting a growth mindset allows you to learn, adapt, and come back stronger. Here's what that looks like in action:

- **Consider failure as a lesson:** When things don't go as planned, swap *I failed.* for *What's my next move?* It's you who judge yourself, not failure. Failure is simply a nudge toward growth, adjustment, and an even better outcome.
- **Talk about it:** If someone said, "Yeah, I bombed my first interview too," or "I've failed my driver's test twice," wouldn't that make things feel way less isolating? The more we talk about struggle, the more normal it becomes.
- **Keep going:** You can either let fear stop you, or you can wear it like a badge of honor—proof that you care enough to push yourself. You only fail when you quit trying; everything else is a lesson.

Vulnerability as Strength

Staying in a cozy bubble can keep you from experiencing the thrill of new adventures and the satisfaction of overcoming challenges. Moreover, research shows that when we experience failure, our brains are forced to analyze, adjust, and problem-solve, which leads to deeper learning and improvement. This is known as productive failure, and it's how some of the world's most successful people got where they are today (Kapur & Bielaczyc, 2012).

However, it's important to note that the benefits of productive failure are most evident when individuals actively reflect on their mistakes and extract meaningful lessons from them. Otherwise, the lessons failure offers can go unnoticed.

Also keep in mind that growth doesn't happen in your comfort zone, but neither does it thrive in total panic mode. The sweet spot for learning is right in between—where you're challenged but not drowning. It means the best way to learn is to push yourself past what you already know, but not so far that you feel completely lost. My advice? If you feel frustrated but still curious, you're in the right spot. If you're on the verge of a meltdown, take a step back and look for a smaller challenge meantime.

Fun Fact #6:

It only takes one person to start a "psychological safety cascade." One moment of honesty, one real conversation, and eventually, the whole group feels safer to be themselves.

Leaning on Strengths

A lot of people get stuck focusing on their weaknesses—what they can't do, what they struggle with, what they wish they were better at. But why waste time obsessing over what you lack when you've got strengths that others don't? Every person is wired differently for a reason—your strengths are your competitive edge. They're the areas where you can outperform with less effort, where you can shine while others grapple, where you can innovate while others imitate. No one gets successful by being "kind of good" at everything —they succeed by being *great* at something specific.

A fish doesn't need to climb trees to prove its worth—it excels where it's meant to. You're already equipped with everything you need to make it—you just need to recognize it and play to it. So, what's one thing you do effortlessly that others have a hard time doing? Look within and bring that to light.

Good Communication: Are You a Natural at Expressing Yourself?

- Do people come to you for advice because you actually know what to say?
- Are you that friend who always smooths over drama before it explodes?
- Can you explain things in a way that makes sense, even when the topic is complicated?

How to use it: Strong communication skills can take you far—use them to lead, resolve conflicts, advocate for yourself, or perhaps crush a future TED Talk.

Friendliness: Do You Make People Feel Comfortable?

- Do you naturally start conversations with new people without making it awkward?
- Can you turn a room full of strangers into a room full of friends?
- Do people say you have "good energy" or a "positive vibe"?

How to use it: Friendliness is a valuable asset for networking, building strong relationships, and making an impact wherever you go.

Helpfulness: Are You the Problem-Solver in Your Circle?

- Is lending a hand something that comes naturally, even before it's asked for?
- Are you the go-to person when people need help with school, projects or life in general?

- Do you feel really good when you're able to make someone's day easier?

How to use it: Helping others builds leadership skills, emotional intelligence, and strong social bonds; plus, it's scientifically proven to boost happiness.

Leadership: Who Steps Up When Things Get Tough?

- Do you find yourself leading the charge when things need organizing?
- Are you good at making quick, smart decisions?
- Can you manage a group without losing your mind?

Multitasking: Can You Handle a Lot at Once?

- Handling homework, texts, and music without missing a beat—how does that work?
- School, friends, hobbies, and responsibilities all lined up and running smoothly—how do you pull it off?
- Are you the type who always has 10 tabs open—literally and metaphorically?

How to use it: Multitasking can be a powerful skill, but only if used wisely—prioritizing, not overloading yourself! Employers and leaders love people who can juggle multiple things without dropping the ball.

Creativity: How Often Do You Find Yourself Brainstorming New Ideas?

- Do you see the world differently?
- Are you the one in group projects who suggests something totally outside the box?

- Have you ever thought, *I should probably write that down* because your brain is bursting with ideas?

How to use it: Creativity is a game-changer in almost every field—whether it's business, art, tech, or problem-solving. Use it to innovate and stand out!

Physical Strength: Are You Resilient in More Ways Than One?

- Can you push yourself physically—sports, fitness, endurance?
- Do you feel strong, both in body and mindset?
- Challenging yourself physically—how often do you go beyond what you thought you could do?

How to use it: Physical strength builds mental strength. It teaches resilience, discipline, and endurance—qualities that make champions, in sports and life.

As we wrap things up, remember that your strengths are not separate little boxes you check off on some life skills list. They flow together, mix and match, and create an awesome combination that makes you uniquely you. Maybe your version of leadership looks different from your friend's, or your way of being creative wouldn't win in any art shows but could totally revolutionize how your school's recycling program works.

There's no right way to be strong, except your own. Given that, you don't need to copy someone else's version of strong. All that matters is seeing the power in yourself and using it in your own way. And for the record, the world better get ready, because a girl who knows her own strength is unstoppable.

Key Takeaways:

• Fear is proof that you're pushing your limits—it's the price of greatness.

• The only people who don't fail are the ones who never try —don't let that be you.

• You can't shut your amygdala off, but you can train your brain to see mistakes as opportunities instead of threats.

• Most fears are just shadows—they vanish when you walk away with something even better—experience.

• The moments when you feel most exposed are likely the ones when you're most capable of growth.

• You don't have to be good at everything—you just have to know what you are good at.

• Be prepared to go all in and crush it...or fail spectacularly trying. Either way, you're winning.

4

OVERCOMING NEGATIVE SELF-TALK AND INNER CRITIC

T houghts have a way of repeating themselves. They bounce around in your mind, growing louder with each echo, until a small thought turns into a big one. This is the power of self-talk—the endless conversation you have with yourself that no one else can hear but everyone experiences.

Scientists have allegedly claimed that the average person has between 12,000 and 60,000 thoughts a day, though what they haven't mentioned is how many of those thoughts might actually be working against them (Burket, n.d.).

In the maze of adolescence, where every turn seems to raise another question about who you are and who you're becoming, these thoughts take on a life of their own. They become the narrators of your story, the commentators of your daily life, and sometimes— more often than you'd like to admit—your harshest critics.

Undeniably, you can't log off from your thoughts, especially the negative ones. They're there when you wake up, they follow you through the day, and they're often the last thing you hear before you fall asleep. Their scripts may be written in invisible ink, but their impact is anything but invisible. You see it in the hesitation before raising your hand in class, in the decision to skip the tryouts, and in the moments when you hold back your ideas, fearing judgment or failure.

But don't worry—just because your mind is always buzzing doesn't mean you're stuck with every thought it throws at you, especially when some thoughts are helpful, others... not so much. You have the ability to decide which ones matter and which ones don't. In this chapter, we'll examine how to tune in, sort through the noise, and start creating a more supportive headspace—without all the extra pressure.

THE TRUTH ABOUT YOUR THOUGHTS

Your brain "lies" to you—not because it's mean or trying to sabotage you, but because that's literally its job. Every second of every day, your brain filters out countless pieces of information to keep you functioning (Zimmerman, 1989). It fills in gaps, makes assumptions, and sometimes flat-out invents things—all while convincing you that everything it tells you is absolutely true (Loftus, 1993).

In fact, our brains evolve for efficiency rather than accuracy. To handle the millions of sensory inputs it receives each second, your brain selectively focuses on what's most important (Zimmerman, 1989). For example, there's a literal blind spot in your vision, but your brain smooths it over like, *Nothing to see here!*—and you'd never even notice. It also loves shortcuts, using your past experiences and biases to make snap judgments (Kahneman, 2011). Firmly, that helps you react fast, but it can also mess things up when it comes to what you see, remember, and decide. Yep, sometimes your brain straight-up lies to you about your own memories!

Long story short, your thoughts aren't always facts, even though they feel like they are. Think about that for a second. Every time you think *I'm not good enough* or *Everyone is judging me*, your brain is presenting these thoughts as breaking news headlines, complete with flashing lights and sirens. But in reality, they're more like rough drafts—messy, incomplete, and usually way off the mark, which often need serious fast-checking and editing.

Neuroscientists have identified several common thought distortions —ways our brains twist reality—that almost everyone experiences. However, teenagers tend to encounter them more intensely due to internal and external factors.

Internally, your brain's already in a hormonal chaos, and those changes crank up your emotions big time. This can make those negative thoughts feel extra intense and overwhelming (Blakemore, 2018). And then, just to keep things interesting (not really), there's social media. It puts fuel on the fire, flooding you with highlight reels of everyone else's seemingly "perfect" lives. Your brain, already biased toward quick assumptions, sees these posts and starts screaming, *See? You're not doing enough! You don't measure up!* What a drama queen, right?

Fun Fact #7:

FOMO (Fear of Missing Out) is pretty common—everyone's having fun while you're left wondering if you should've also gone out. But JOMO (Joy of Missing Out) flips that on its head. It's all about enjoying your own company, Netflix binge included. No shame in staying in!

So, what are these pesky patterns your brain tends to fall for? Let's take a look at a few big ones:

The Spotlight Effect

We've all had that legendary cafeteria trip—where your foot betrayed you, and you thought the whole world was watching in slow motion. *OMG, I'll never live this down! Everyone saw that, and they're all judging me!* Nope. They probably didn't.

Funny enough, most people are too caught up worrying about their own lives to obsess over your stumble. Some might not even notice, and those who do? They'll forget it faster than you think. Everyone's got their own mental stage where they think they're the star of the show. You're starring in "The Life of You" and someone else is starring in "The Life of Them." They aren't extras in your movie—they're too busy focusing on their next scene.

So, the next time your brain starts screaming, *Everyone's watching me!* tell it to chill. At the end of the day, no one's replaying your cafeteria trip in their head like you are—well, except maybe you!

The All-Or-Nothing Trap

All-or-nothing thinking locks you into a rigid, black-and-white mindset—you're either a total success or a complete failure. This thought trap is common in anxiety, depression, and perfectionism (Beck, 1976). It makes you blow one setback out of proportion. One bad grade turns into, "I failed that quiz, so I'm obviously terrible at this subject forever."

Obviously, life doesn't work that way. Success and failure aren't all-or-nothing; they live on a spectrum. You may be far from being a genius, but you're not doomed. You're not the life of the party, but neither are you a ghost. You're not a brainiac, but you're not hopeless either. There are wins, setbacks, retries, and tons of gray areas in between—but your brain sometimes refuses to acknowledge them!

Fun Fact #8:

Are you waiting for the "perfect time" to do something? Well, I hate to burst your bubble, but that moment may never come. The universe isn't going to send you a neon sign that says, "Now's the time!" Perfectionism tricks us into thinking to wait for that "magical moment" before we act, but the truth is, it's about showing up and taking action.

Mind Reading

Have you ever caught yourself playing psychic? You know, that thing where someone doesn't text back and you're absolutely convinced they hate you, they're mad at you, or they're sitting there thinking about how weird that thing you said last week was. Congratulations! You've discovered your brain's secret superpower: mind reading! Disappointingly, it's not as cool as it sounds. Why? Because everyone else is too busy mind-reading about themselves to be thinking about what you think they're thinking about you.

One of the coolest tricks your brain plays is figuring out what others are thinking—a process called "theory of mind," and it's vital for connecting with people (Premack & Woodruff, 1978). However, in your teenage years, this ability is in overdrive, constantly analyzing everyone's thoughts but not yet great at avoiding those "too-quick" conclusions (Blakemore, 2018).

Unless you actually have supernatural powers, you can't really read minds. You can, however, do the following:

- Recognize when you're making assumptions.
- Question those assumptions.
- Consider other possibilities.

- Ask for clarification when possible.

All in all, whenever the brain tries to convince you it knows exactly what someone else is thinking, remind it that even real psychics get it wrong sometimes. And as incredible as your brain is, it's not actually psychic—it's simply skilled at crafting stories. Besides, if mind reading were real, wouldn't someone have aced every test they took? Something to think about.

The Fortune Teller Error

You've probably never been to a fortune teller, but chances are you're secretly great at predicting the future—or at least, your brain thinks it is.

Your brain loves convincing you that it can predict the future, usually the worst possible one. *If I speak up in class, everyone will think I'm stupid.* Your brain jumps straight to the worst possible outcome, adds some special effects, and presents it to you as a documentary rather than the fiction it actually is.

How many times has your brain predicted complete disaster, only for things to turn out pretty okay? Would you believe that most of your worries are lying to you? That's what Don Joseph Goewey discovered. As the author of the bestseller "The End of Stress" and head of the human performance firm ProAttitude, he revealed that 80% of our worrying thoughts never actually come true.

But wait, it gets even better. Out of the 15% of worries that actually did come true (you know, the real-life stuff), there are two surprising things:

- Either people handled the situation way better than they thought they would.
- They learned something really valuable from the experience.

This means that 97% of the time, your worries are just your brain running a very dramatic simulation of things that either won't happen or aren't nearly as bad as you think they'll be (Goewey, 2015). Your brain might think it has a crystal ball—a fancy tool it uses to "prepare" you for the worst. It believes that if you're ready for every disaster, it can somehow protect you from pain. That said, the future is still a blank page. And even if someone had scribbled on it, who says you can't grab an eraser and write your own version? You're in charge of your life's plot twists, not your brain's fear-based fantasies.

Don't get me wrong, though. I'm not suggesting you ignore your thoughts completely. Some worries do have a purpose—they're little mental alarms trying to protect you from real danger. You don't want to ignore the voice telling you, *It's best to not walk through that dark alley alone.* The key is being your own detective and figuring out which alarms are real and which are just overreactions. Stick around, because up next, I'll show you how to start cracking the case!

__Fun Fact #9:__

Your brain is often set to "worst-case scenario" mode, but it also comes with an "optimism filter" that can be turned on. Switch it on, and you'll start noticing the bright side.

BREAKING FREE FROM NEGATIVE SELF-TALK

Self-talk is tied to how you process the world around you. Your thoughts influence your emotions, which in turn influence your actions. No wonder then that negative self-talk can become a self-fulfilling prophecy. If you keep telling yourself you're not good enough, you might actually end up believing it. And when you believe something, you act on it. The cycle continues, making it harder to break out. Nevertheless, you can reprogram your brain. With enough practice, you can literally rewire it to be more positive and less prone to negative thinking. Here's how:

Challenge Your Thoughts

When you catch yourself thinking something negative, ask yourself these questions:

- *What actual evidence do we have?*
- *Has this witness (worry) been reliable in the past?*
- *Are there other possible explanations?*
- *Could we be jumping to conclusions?*

This process is known as cognitive restructuring—a fancy way of saying, "Let's take a closer look at what's really going on here" (Beck, 1976).

For example, instead of thinking, *I'm horrible at math, I'll never get it,* challenge that thought with, *Did I do well in math before? Did I struggle with other subjects and overcame it?* Think about the 99 times you succeeded, not the one time you didn't; then swap those negative thoughts for more realistic ones and see how it can completely change your mindset and mood.

The Three-Step Thought Reset:

1. Catch the critical thought.

2. Challenge it with evidence.

3. Replace it with a more balanced perspective.

Shift Your Focus to the Present

Every time you notice your mind drifting to past regrets or future anxieties, try to dial it back and zero in on what's happening right now. Why does this matter? The present moment carries an unrivaled strength that neither the past nor the future can match: It's real. You can touch it, feel it, and interact with it. It's the only time you truly have any power. It's where you can take action, make choices, and create change. Your mind may be a time machine, but your life can only be lived now. Plus, it stops you from being stuck in a loop of "what ifs" and "could have beens."

The idea is straightforward: Stop for a second. Take a breath. Look around you. Take a deep breath, and let the world around you come into focus. You might notice the breeze brushing past, the soft fabric of your hoodie, or even the quiet hum of your surroundings. Alternatively, try something physical—stand up and stretch, take a walk around, or maybe even do a quick, silly dance move. The point is, break the loop with awareness. Sometimes, a slight shift is enough to break free from a negative thought spiral.

A Few Other Ways to Stay Present:

- **Create a "right now" playlist with your favorite upbeat songs.**

- **Take a mindful walk and notice all the colors around you.**

- **Take silly selfies with your pet.**

- **Draw or doodle whatever catches your eye.**

Surround Yourself With Positivity

Never again in your life will you be so powerfully shaped by your social environment. Each day, intentional or not, you make choices about what influences your mind. The social media accounts you follow, the conversations you have, the relationships you maintain, the music you listen to—each of these either supports your growth or brings negativity into your life.

Consider your phone—that little device you check a whopping 9 hours a day—yes, that's the actual average for teenagers (Zauderer, 2023). Every time you unlock it, you're opening a door to an endless flow of information. What's coming through? Is it positive, motivating, uplifting content, or is it full of comparisons, judgment, and unrealistic standards?

More often than not, it's the latter. Social media algorithms are designed to keep you scrolling, showing you what grabs your attention and keeps you engaged—but not necessarily what's good for you. YouTube videos have been around long enough (from 2004) that viewers can recognize they're being created for cloud and click-bait purposes. The issue is, you'll keep being fed popular content. Celebrity drama, unrealistic beauty standards, and that perfect #NoFilter lifestyle—they all pop up on your feed uninvited. Forget meaningful connections and inspiration—because here, it's all about comparing your behind-the-scenes to someone else's highlight reel. Staying informed is important, but how much anxiety can your brain handle? Too much negativity can trick you into thinking the future is hopeless.

The people you meet either lift you up or bring you down, too. That's because, on a biological level, your stress hormones, happiness chemicals, and thought patterns can mirror the people around you. Recall a time you spent with someone who couldn't stop complaining. How did you feel afterward? Now think about time spent with someone who radiates enthusiasm and possibility. Different feeling, isn't it?

So, what's next? Unfollow accounts that leave you feeling inadequate, even if they're popular. I'm not really concerned with how much time you spend online as long as you're intentional about what you let into your mind; everything is fair game.

Also, don't waste your time on friends who deplete you, no matter how long you've known them. When it comes to family who might have that same effect, cutting them out isn't always an option, but setting healthy boundaries is. And make sure you're balancing that by surrounding yourself with people who recharge your spirit.

Adjust your routine to include elements that enrich your mental soil as well—be it meditation, journaling, or physical movement. No room for excuses here—if you prioritize it, you'll always find time.

Advantageously, you can't control every aspect of your social environment, but you can be strategic about the parts within your control. The activities you invest in, the content you consume, and who you build relationships with—they're all in your hands. These decisions might feel small now, but they'll mold how you experience the world for years to come. Ergo, choose wisely!

Add "Yet" to Your Vocabulary

Take any limiting thought you've had today and add "yet" to the end of it. That sentence stops being an ending and turns into a new beginning.

- "I can't do this... yet."
- "I can't understand chemistry... yet."
- "I'm not confident speaking in front of people... yet."
- "I can't cook eggs without breaking the yolk... yet."

When we say "I'm not good at this," our brain treats it as a fact, like saying "the sky is blue" or "water is wet." It's done, settled, case closed. But using "yet" shifts that mindset, signaling to your brain that your skills are still developing and that you're in progress, not stuck. It encourages you to explore new strategies, keep trying, and believe that improvement is possible—as long as you put in the effort.

Absolutely, you're not denying the current reality. If something's hard, it's hard. "Yet" just keeps you from seeing that difficulty as permanent. Instead of being the person who "can't do math," you become the person who's "working on getting better at math." And for me, "yet" is proof that I'm still growing, still learning, still moving forward.

However, not everything needs a "yet." "I can't fly without wings... yet" certainly isn't worth your energy (unless you're secretly developing jet pack technology). The true strength of "yet" shines through in situations where

- the skill is learnable.
- you seriously want to improve.
- it's something within human possibility.
- you're willing to put in the work.

The journey from "nope" to "hope" is just three letters long. So, what if this strategy feels awkward at first? Well, you're not comfortable with it... yet.

Key Takeaways:

- **Your thoughts can be your BFF or your worst enemy since they're _not always_ true.**

• No one's watching your every move—seriously, no one cares that much. Focus on your own scene.

• Your brain's future predictions? Pure fiction.

• Mind Reading = Nope. Stop assuming you know what others are thinking.

• "What ifs" are the past's way of messing with your head. Get back to today; make it count!

• Everything that grows in your mind is the result of the environment you create within it.

• Choose vibes that energize you. You're not a battery; don't let anything drain you.

5
PEER PRESSURE TO CONFORM AND STRESS

Teenage girls making countless tiny tweaks throughout their day isn't an unusual thing. A walk modified to the right amount of confidence. An opinion softened to avoid rocking the boat. An interest hidden to fit the mold. A dream scaled back to meet expectations. No one asked for these adjustments. No one commanded them. Yet they happen automatically.

These tiny compromises seem harmless in the moment. What's wrong with turning down your music when others give you that look? What's the big deal about pretending you don't love that "uncool" movie? Why not wear what everyone else is wearing? But the catch is, they add up. One held-back opinion becomes a pattern of always keeping quiet. One concealed interest turns into a constant act of fitting in. One scaled-back dream becomes a lifetime of wondering *What if?*

The pressure to conform isn't new—it's as old as human society itself. What's new is the intensity. Between Instagram, TikTok, Snapchat, and whatever new platform dropped while I was writing this sentence, you're dealing with more pressure than any generation before. Your mom might talk about how hard high school was in her day or how she had to dodge the neighborhood gossip, but she didn't have to maintain a perfect social media presence while doing it. Meanwhile, you're handling peer pressure from every corner of the globe 24/7. And it doesn't relate to just clothes or music anymore but to your entire existence.

Care about issues, but not too intensely. Be ambitious, but not threatening. Be confident, but not arrogant. Be yourself, but make sure that self fits within acceptable parameters. The result?—stress levels in teenage girls hitting historic highs! The pressure to conform while simultaneously standing out (try making sense of that paradox!) is messing with young brains. Your generation is experiencing anxiety rates that would have been unthinkable twenty years ago.

THE PRESSURE'S REAL

Peer pressure is the influence that people in your social circle have on your decisions, behavior, and beliefs. It doesn't just mean being told directly, "You have to do this," though that's definitely one form. It can also be more indirect, like feeling like you should go along with something because everyone else is doing it.

Why is peer pressure so powerful? One word: belonging. We all have a deep-rooted need to belong to a group. That craving to be seen, connected, and understood is built into our DNA because we've evolved to rely on others for survival. This, as a result, makes it almost impossible to say "no" when the group expects you to go along with something—even when your gut is whispering, *Nah, not for me.*

Peer pressure can further come from a place of fear or insecurity. When everyone around you is doing something, there's this feeling that maybe you're the odd one out if you don't do it too. Obviously, no one wants to be the one standing on the outside, not laughing at the joke, or skipping the invitation. And with everything else going on—school stress, social anxiety, and trying to survive the ups and downs of being a teen—peer pressure appears as a safety blanket you're tempted to grab onto. Right now, your brain could be focused on fitting in, leaving the consequences for later.

Fun Fact #10:

Interacting with avatars tricks your brain into feeling included. It's why virtual friendships can ease loneliness and digital hangouts feel so genuine. Your mind isn't picky about what's real or virtual—it just wants connection. Could this be a new tool for tackling social anxiety?

TYPES OF PEER PRESSURE: POSITIVE VS. NEGATIVE

Most people hear about peer pressure and picture some shady friend tempting you with, "Just one puff, nobody will know." But peer pressure isn't always the villain twirling its mustache in the corner. It can also be a powerful motivator to make good choices. Knowing which one you're being steered toward makes all the difference.

Positive Peer Pressure

Let's start with the good news: peer pressure that always pushes you to do the right thing. Got a friend who loves working out and invites you to come along? Or a classmate who's super into volunteering and convinces you to help out? That's positive peer pressure in its purest form, not a force that urges you to conform, but an environment that inspires you to grow.

One of the most powerful aspects of positive peer pressure is its authenticity. Unlike negative pressure, which often requires you to become less of yourself, positive pressure encourages you to become more of who you are. No masks, no pretensions. It doesn't push you to dim your light to fit in; it challenges you to shine even brighter. In the end, every time you overcome a challenge, no matter how small, you gain confidence—each win stacking up until the impossible starts to feel achievable.

Best of all, you don't have to climb that mountain alone. Positive peer groups pull each other up. They uncover strengths you didn't realize you have in you and build new ones along the way. In the right environment, striving for excellence is a shared journey.

So, how do you build that kind of supportive environment?

- **Choose or lose**

They weren't lying when they said, "You are who you hang out with." Wanna stay lazy? Chill with slackers. Wanna win? Surround yourself with hustlers. It's that simple. When your friends are out there chasing dreams, you'll feel that same itch to go after yours. So pick people who hype you up, set big goals, and own their mistakes like champs. No settling for meh vibes.

At the same time, don't be afraid to distance yourself from people who constantly drag you down. You can still care about them without letting their negative influence dictate your choices.

- **Set the standard**

Positive pressure works both ways. If you want to be part of a group that lifts each other up, you've got to bring that same energy. Be the friend who encourages others to chase their dreams, work through challenges, and stay true to themselves. Celebrate their wins—no shade, no envy. When everyone feels valued and supported, the whole group thrives.

Interestingly enough, the energy you put out will come back to you. That's how strong friendships are built.

- **Learn to give and receive feedback**

For positive peer pressure to work, open communication is essential. That means you have to be comfortable giving and receiving feedback. Real friends will call you out when you're slacking, but in a way that makes you feel motivated, not judged. Similarly, you should be able to offer constructive criticism without tearing anyone down. A foundation of trust and honest feedback helps everyone grow together.

To set the distinction, not all criticism is the same—there's a sharp contrast between humiliating criticism and constructive criticism. Consider a group project scenario: A team member has missed several deadlines. The natural frustration might lead to words that cut deep: "You're clearly not taking this seriously. You're letting everyone down, as usual." This harsh reproach attacks not just the person's work but also their character, instilling shame rather than motivation.

In contrast, constructive criticism frames the same situation differently: "I've noticed the deadlines have been challenging to meet. This is impacting our team's progress, but I believe we can find a way to make this work better. Could we discuss what obstacles you're facing?" This approach maintains dignity while addressing the issue at hand.

Negative Peer Pressure

Sadly, negative peer pressure is everywhere—it's often the first thing that comes to mind when we hear the term. This is the kind of pressure that pushes you to fit in at any cost, even if it means going against your values, risking your health, or sacrificing your happiness. The worst part is that you willingly go along with it for fear of being left out or judged.

Negative peer pressure doesn't always look the same. Sometimes, it's loud and in-your-face. Other times, it's more like an invisible current pulling you along. And occasionally, you might even create that pressure in your own mind. To handle it, you need to understand how it works.

- **Direct pressure**

This is the in-your-face version of peer pressure, and it's exactly what you picture in those after-school specials. Someone comes at you with a challenge, a taunt, or a so-called "friendly suggestion" that's not so friendly.

- "Everyone's doing it."
  - "What, don't tell me you're scared?"
  - "Don't be such a loser."

Direct pressure can be sneaky when it comes wrapped in jokes or casual comments. Someone might laugh while they're pressuring you, making you feel like you're overreacting if you take it seriously. But make no mistake—the pressure is real. These people want you to feel uncomfortable and self-conscious. They aim to embarrass you and nudge you into doing what they want, exploiting your natural fear of standing out.

- **Indirect pressure**

This type of pressure uses the power of numbers to make you doubt yourself. In simpler terms, it's not one person telling you what to do; it's the group's energy slowly influencing your decisions.

Even adults cave to group pressure; just look at the ones who panic-buy the latest phone they don't really need. So, thinking teens can ignore it is wishful thinking at best.

Group pressure is particularly dangerous because it makes bad choices feel... well, not so bad. Repeated behavior in your circle can turn risky actions into something that seems ordinary, or even expected.

- **Self-imposed pressure**

Weird, right? You can pressure yourself without anyone else saying a word. After being exposed to external pressure for so long, you start internalizing it. You become your own toughest critic, constantly policing your thoughts and actions. You second-guess your choices, holding yourself to unrealistic standards that aren't even yours. It's a relentless mental loop that convinces you these expectations are your own. But in reality, they're leftover baggage from the peer pressure you've been exposed to.

On a more pragmatic note, living under constant pressure—whether from others or yourself—will slowly but surely build up stress. And honestly, how could it not? You're constantly stuck in your head, worrying about others' opinions, chasing impossible standards, and freaking out over the smallest missteps. Exhausting? Anyone would be. Absolutely draining.

WHAT STRESS DOES TO YOU: INSIDE YOUR BODY AND MIND

Under stress, your brain releases a flood of chemicals, mainly cortisol (the main stress hormone) and adrenaline (the fight-or-flight hormone). Cortisol gets your body ready to deal with stress by increasing sugar levels in your bloodstream to provide quick energy. It also lowers inflammation in the body and alters your immune response—getting you ready for what's next, whether that's running away or dealing with the situation head-on.

Adrenaline, on the other hand, is your body's quick-response mode. When your body senses danger, it floods your system with adrenaline. In the short term, this is pretty impressive engineering. Your body is literally preparing you to either fight off a threat or run away from it (hence the term "fight-or-flight response"). Your pupils dilate to see better, your breathing quickens to get more oxygen, and your digestive system temporarily shuts down because, to be honest, digesting lunch isn't a priority when you're in danger.

That said, these protective hormones can turn against you if stress sticks around too long, causing physical and emotional challenges. For girls, this imbalance can even hit harder.

Gender Differences in Stress Experience

Girls' brains tend to crank out more cortisol than guys' when they're stressed, and that can make anxiety go through the roof. Plus, girls are more likely to focus inward when stressed—worrying about their appearance, friendships, and social status. This internalization often leads to rumination—the act of obsessively thinking about negative thoughts and feelings—which can make stress feel endless.

In contrast, boys are more likely to externalize stress, often acting out or showing frustration outwardly. Instead of worrying excessively or withdrawing, they may express anger or take a more "fight" approach to stress.

Because girls normally process stress internally, their reactions can appear more emotional than boys' reactions. But due to gendered expectations and stereotypes, people usually underestimate this issue. The cycle of minimizing and misunderstanding girls' stress leads to an even deeper issue: internalized shame. When girls are told, "You're overreacting" or "Stop being dramatic," they begin to internalize the message that their feelings are not important. This builds internalized shame, making them less likely to reach out for help when they really need it. The more they bottle it up, the harder it hits their mental health later on.

Long-term Effects of Stress

If stress is left unchecked, it doesn't disappear on its own, which can result in:

- **Mental health disorders:** Constant stress can leave you battling anxiety, depression, or post-traumatic stress disorder (PTSD). Without healthy coping skills, your brain can spiral downward, and it's hard to climb out.
- **Physical problems:** Long-term stress has been linked to high blood pressure, heart disease, digestive issues, and weakened immunity (so you catch every cold and flu in sight). This is because cortisol, if it's continuously elevated, can negatively impact various bodily systems.
- **Cognitive decline:** Chronic stress can impair your memory and learning (because your brain's too busy being stressed to store new information effectively)—bad news for a brain that's still growing. Constant pressure can also wreck your ability to make good decisions .

So what does this all mean for you? Simply put, stress isn't something you should ignore. You must take it seriously. Pay attention, check in with yourself, and get the help you need when things get too overwhelming for you.

Self-Assessment: How Stressed Are You?

For each statement, rate how often it applies to you on the following scale:

0 = Never, 1 = Occasionally, 2 = Often, 3 = Almost Always

Section 1: Physical Signs

☐ My energy is gone, and I didn't even spend it.

☐ I usually get headaches or stomachaches.

☐ I have trouble falling asleep or staying asleep.

☐ My muscles feel tense or sore without a clear reason.

☐ My heart sometimes races, or I feel short of breath when stressed.

☐ I feel restless or on edge, like I can't relax.

Section 2: Emotional and Mental Signs

☐ I struggle to manage everything on my plate.

☐ I am constantly anxious or worried.

☐ I get irritated or angry easily, sometimes over small things.

☐ I find it hard to enjoy things I normally like.

☐ I put pressure on myself to be perfect and meet high expectations.

☐ I often overthink or replay negative situations in my head.

Section 3: Cognitive (Thinking) Signs

☐ I find it hard to concentrate and stay focused on tasks.

☐ I forget things I normally wouldn't, like assignments or plans.

☐ I overthink or hesitate when making even small decisions.

☐ My thoughts are scattered, making it hard to think clearly.

Section 4: Behavioral Signs

☐ I withdraw from friends, family, or activities I used to enjoy.

☐ I procrastinate and avoid responsibilities because I feel overwhelmed.

☐ I notice changes in my eating habits (eating too much or too little).

☐ I rely more on distractions like social media or gaming to escape.

☐ I lash out at people or have emotional outbursts when stressed.

☐ I avoid situations that I know will stress me out.

Scoring and Results

1. Add up your points for each section.
2. Find your total score:
   - **0–15 points:** You've got some stress (who doesn't?), but it's nothing you can't handle. You're in a pretty manageable zone right now. Just keep an eye on your habits and make sure you're not ignoring the small stuff.
   - **16–35 points:** Okay, your stress is starting to creep up, and it's weighing you down. Time to hit pause and figure out what's stressing you out.
   - **36+ points:** Whoa, your stress is on high alert. This isn't something to brush off. It might be messing with your mood, sleep, or even your ability to think straight. Time to take action!

Stress-Relief Techniques

Stress sucks, but luckily, science has your back with some go-to techniques to keep your cool when things spiral out of control.

- **Breathe like you mean it (deep breathing)**

Sounds too simple to work, right? But it does. Slow, deep breaths tell your brain, *Hey, we're not being chased by a bear,* and your body follows the lead.

<u>Why it works:</u> Deep breathing reduces cortisol levels and activates your parasympathetic nervous system, which is basically your body's "relax mode."

- **Move your body (exercise)**

Can't run? Don't want to? No problem. Take a quick walk, bust out a 30-second squat, or hit a trending TikTok challenge—Renegade, Wednesday Addams, or whatever's blowing up on your FYP. Get goofy, have fun, and don't sweat the perfection—unless, of course, you're aiming for viral fame.

<u>Why it works:</u> Physical activity releases endorphins—those feel-good chemicals that boost your mood and reduce stress.

- **Laugh it out (Seriously)**

Not in the mood to laugh? Fake it 'til you make it. Watch a funny fail compilation, a stand-up comedy clip, or your favorite rom-com movies. Why, even chuckling can help! Or better yet, call your funniest friend—the one who always has a story that leaves you in stitches.

<u>Why it works:</u> Laughter lowers cortisol, boosts feel-good endorphins, and helps release built-up tension—basically a stress-busting life hack.

- **Snooze to win**

Whoever said only babies need sleep clearly never had to survive a math test on three hours of rest. Lack of sleep turns your brain into a glitchy mess—forgetting things, overreacting, and stressing over that weird text from your crush. Get your 7–9 hours (yes, even during exam season), and you'll handle all that unnecessary drama exceptionally. Trust me, your brain works better when it's not running on fumes.

Why it works: Sleep lowers stress hormones, keeps you from spiraling, and lets your brain catch a break.

- **Talk it out (with someone you trust)**

Don't keep your stress locked up as a top-secret file. Spill it to someone you trust—your BFF, your sibling, a family member, or a therapist. Saying your worries out loud makes things less terrifying. And no, you won't sound "dramatic." Bonus: You might get advice or a pep talk that actually helps.

Why it works: Talking activates the brain's emotional regulation centers, reducing cortisol levels and calming the nervous system. It gives you a fresh perspective on the problem, too.

- **Cut down on caffeine and sugar (Sorry, but it helps)**

Yes, I get it—your double-shot latte or that "just one more" soda is your lifesaver. Disappointingly, caffeine and sugar are sneaky little stress enhancers. Try cutting back; swap that second coffee for herbal tea or water every now and then. No, you don't have to quit completely (I'm not a monster).

Why it works: Caffeine cranks up your heart rate, spikes your anxiety, and sends your sleep schedule packing.

Fun Fact #11:

Your body can crave stress the same way it craves caffeine —except there's no tasty latte, just exhaustion.

BUILDING CONFIDENCE IN THE FACE OF PRESSURE

Most advice about building confidence sounds great, but frankly speaking—they're aren't all that practical. "Act natural!" Great, except when your friends are pressuring you to skip class and you're not even sure who your real self is yet. "Follow your heart"? Sure, but what if your heart can't make up its mind? One second it's urging you to stay true to your values, and the next it's begging you not to draw too much attention. Yeah, that's helpful... not!

So, what's the solution? Definitely not more of the same motivational fluff. You need strategies that actually work when the stakes are high. This section is all about that—practical steps you can count on.

Fun fact #12:

Regular cold exposure—chilled shower, to be exact—toughens up your mind, boosts your confidence, and teaches you to stay cool under pressure—literally. Who knew therapy could come straight from the tap?

Know Your Values

What matters to you? Is it being kind to others? Staying honest even when it's hard? Or you value creativity and want to live life on your own terms. Whatever it is, strong confidence comes from knowing exactly where you stand. While rules tell you **what** to do, values guide you in **why** you do things. They provide the reason behind your decisions, allowing you to trust yourself in any situation. No one needs to tell you right from wrong because you can sense it deep within. That certainty gives you the strength to stand your ground and fight for what matters most.

Above all, your values must be truly yours so that peer pressure can lose its power over you. You can't borrow someone else's values any more than you can borrow their personality. You might share values with your family or friends, but the ones that really stick are the ones you've chosen for yourself. They're the principles you'd stand by even if you were the only one standing.

A great way to lock in your values is to write down three things you'll never compromise on. Not what your parents say, not what your friends think—what YOU believe holds true. Putting your values into writing makes them more real and easier to stick to. Keep the list handy—on your phone or somewhere you'll see it often. Revisit it daily until it becomes part of how you naturally live your life.

Your Ready-Made Exit Strategy

Have three ready-to-go responses for getting out of uncomfortable situations. Make them simple and true: "Not my thing," "Nah, I'm good," or "I've got other stuff going on" works better than any long, dramatic excuse. No need for a five-minute explanation about why you can't join in on a risky plan. You don't owe anyone a reason for saying no.

Most people think they need elaborate stories to get out of uncomfortable situations. They invent sick relatives, forgotten appointments, or sudden emergencies. But these complicated exits often backfire. You end up trapped in your own lie or feel you're doing something *wrong* by leaving, when in reality, you're doing something *right* by honoring your boundaries.

Flip the Pressure

Whenever someone tries to make you feel bad about your choices, flip the script. "Why does this matter so much to you?" puts the pressure back where it belongs—on them.

Psychologically, people rarely expect to be questioned about their motives and often have no real reason for their behavior. Since they aren't ready for this move, such an unexpected question forces them into a moment of discomfort and confusion. Guess who's in control now?

Maintain a composed tone and keep things light—don't ask in a confrontational way. You're not trying to pick a fight but rather calmly turning the situation around. Standing firm with self-assurance keeps you in charge, removing any pressure to justify your actions or choices to anyone.

Key Takeaways:

• Different types of pressure need different responses.

• The right kind of pressure can make you stronger.

• Trying too hard to fit in makes you invisible. The more you blend in, the less people actually see you.

• Your brain might stress out first, but your body never forgets. Headaches, exhaustion, and restless nights? That's just stress keeping score.

• Stress is part of life. Managing it is part of growth. Don't let it overstay its welcome.

• You're not a pre-packaged product—so why try to fit in a box? Be yourself unapologetically; no approval necessary.

• Confidence isn't born; it's built.

• You can't stop the pressure, but you can get smarter about handling it. Your move.

6

EMOTIONAL REGULATION

I n Greek mythology, Hera was the queen of the gods—powerful, regal, and commanded respect from all. Yet even sitting on her divine throne couldn't save her from the rage that ate her alive.

As Zeus's wife, she endured endless betrayals as he pursued affair after affair, leaving a trail of demigod children that served as constant reminders of his infidelity.

Hera's fury is always nuclear. However, instead of dealing with Zeus (you know, the actual problem), she went after everyone else. She drove Hercules so mad he killed his own family. She forced Leto to wander endlessly, heavily pregnant with nowhere to give birth. She turned Callisto into a literal bear, separating her from her kid. All that divine power, and what did she do with it? Turned it into her own personal revenge machine.

More dramatically, being immortal meant this anger fest never ended. Hera had got the power to do literally anything, be anything, create whole worlds if she wanted to, but instead she just sat up there on Olympus, scrolling through Zeus's divine DMs and plotting her next revenge scheme. No timeout, no moving on, no "new year, new me," no "thanks for the lesson, moving on now!" She stayed stuck in her own fury loop FOREVER, turning her queen-of-the-gods status into her own personal prison. And to clarify, FOREVER was not simply a long time—FOREVER forever. She kept getting back at someone who wasn't even the one who hurt her. If that's not the most terrifying cautionary tale about letting anger win, I don't know what is (Madeleine, 2019; Gilham, 2019).

Okay, I get it—what does Hera have to do with you? You are not an immortal goddess stuck with keeping track of your husband's "extra-curricular activities" (thankfully), and your biggest conflict might be a fight with a friend or a bad grade. But, in all honesty, we've all had Hera moments.

Throughout life, you spend countless hours in school learning algebra, memorizing historical dates, and perfecting your social media posts. Yet, when real emotional challenges arise, you're hardly ever prepared. How do you handle the sting of loneliness when your best friend starts spending more time with someone else? How do you face the frustration and disappointment of failing a test you worked so hard for? And how do you maintain your composure when the person you've secretly admired finally notices you, only for you to freeze up and forget how to even speak? These are moments that hit unexpectedly, and they remind you how vulnerable you are to your feelings.

The bright side is that there are tools to win them, starting with learning how to take control of your emotions. Let's get into it.

Fun Fact #13:

Callisto, the bear-lady, is still in the sky. After Hera turned Callisto into a bear, Zeus felt bad and turned her into a constellation—Ursa Major (the Big Dipper). So basically,

every time you look up at the stars, you're seeing Hera's unresolved jealousy issues.

SELF-AWARENESS: GETTING TO KNOW YOUR EMOTIONAL SELF

Self-awareness is the first step toward emotional regulation. It's about noticing and allowing yourself the space to understand what's happening within you so that emotions don't control you—you control them. Most of the time, emotions do not appear suddenly. They're triggered by something specific—an event, a conversation, or an internal thought. Your challenge is to recognize them as they begin—not after they have already shaped your behavior. The sooner you do, the more control you have over how you respond, which is the foundation for better relationships, smarter decisions, and a stronger, more confident you.

In the words of the 13th-century Persian poet Rumi, "Your task is not to seek for love, but merely to seek and find all the barriers within yourself that you have built against it." This speaks to the heart of self-awareness. Yet for me, this is the most challenging process.

Humans are pretty incredible—we are able to notice and analyze all sorts of things at once! You could be fuming with anger but still secretly know you're being dramatic. Or maybe you're sad and feel like the world is crumbling, but at the same time, you're like, *Hmm, this pain might actually be teaching me something deep...or maybe I'm just hungry.*

The problem, however, is that we don't give ourselves a second to do it. Life doesn't wait, and so do our thoughts and emotions. A sharp word escapes, a door slams, or our chest tightens with anxiety. Only after the moment passes do we pause and think, *Why did I react that way?* But by then, the damage often has been done.

True self-awareness demands precious pause—a space between *feeling* and *reacting*, a moment to catch yourself before your emotions run the show. Since you're resisting emotional momentum, being present enough to ask those questions may not come easily at first. But don't fret—balance is something you already have; it's a matter of practice. And if you ask me where to begin, my take would be the following:

- **Check in with yourself regularly**

Throughout the day, take a moment to ask yourself, *How am I feeling right now? What's going on inside me?* Even when everything things feel...nothing (I mean, you're not sad, but you're not exactly happy either. You're just kind of... there), that's still something worth paying attention to. Getting used to these small self-checks builds a habit of being present, which makes it a lot easier to tune into your emotions.

Not only does routinely checking in with yourself boost your emotional awareness, it also helps you spot patterns and triggers and how your emotions shift at certain moments. Why do you get that sinking feeling as soon as you hit the front door after school? Keep checking in with yourself, and you'll probably figure it out soon enough.

- **Learn to name your emotions**

Good. Bad. Fine. For many of us, that's the extent of our emotional vocabulary—a simplistic set of labels we learned as children and never bothered (or dared) to go beyond them.

Emotions are way more complex than a basic mood chart. There are so many variations, and until you recognize the difference, it's difficult to know what step to take next. Saying "I feel bad" isn't enough —bad how? Are you disappointed, frustrated, hurt, anxious, or overwhelmed? Can't put your finger on it? That's how emotions keep you guessing. Disappointment hits when your expectations aren't met. Frustration comes from feeling stuck. Anxiety is fear about what's ahead, and overwhelm is that drowning sense of too much coming at you at once.

These emotions might all feel negative, but they come from different places, and treating them the same won't get you anywhere. You can't fix what you don't understand. The right solution depends on the right diagnosis—otherwise, you're tossing a multivitamin at a flu that's tearing through your system. If luck is on your side, you'll scrape by. If not, well... let's say wishful thinking won't lower a raging fever, and ignoring the real problem won stop it from getting worse.

Looking back at why we rarely push past the surface of our emotions, the reason is simple: We're afraid to face what's within us. How many times have you said "I'm fine" when someone asked how you were doing, even though you felt far from it? Isn't it strange how we've normalized our emotional shorthand? We'll spend twenty minutes describing the perfect cup of coffee but sum up our entire emotional state with a mere "fine."

"Fine" is much easier. It's our emotional fast food—quick, convenient, and socially acceptable. You don't need to unpack anything, don't have to explain yourself, and most importantly, you avoid having to face whatever emotional turmoil might be bubbling up. That said, it is never truly satisfying and offers about as much nourishment as a flimsy paper wrapper.

We only fear what we cannot name. Hence, the easiest way to move forward is to face your emotions head-on. Know when "fine" is an honest expression and when it's a way of pushing your feelings aside. Be honest with yourself. If you constantly tell yourself you're fine, you begin to disconnect from your own feelings. Our emotions don't actually care if we acknowledge them or not; they're still there.

They wait until they can't be suppressed any longer, and when they finally emerge, they can surprise you, usually in ways you least anticipate.

- **Tracking your cycles**

Understanding your emotions becomes easier when you recognize how they connect to your body's natural rhythms. As you've discovered, hormonal changes create patterns that affect how you experience and process emotions. So, pay attention to how your emotional state fluctuates throughout the day and month. Do you feel more emotionally balanced at certain times or more prone to stress at others? Recognizing these shifts gives you the ability to regulate your emotions better. When you know you're entering a more emotionally sensitive period, you can prepare yourself in advance.

- **Reflect on your reactions**

Think about the last time you got angry or upset. Did you snap at someone? Or did you shut down and avoid talking to them altogether? Now, look deeper. What was really going on? Were you feeling stressed before the situation even started? Were there other things you hadn't dealt with that day that contributed to your reaction? Sometimes, the way you respond to a situation isn't about the event itself but how you were feeling before, during, and after. Reflecting on these moments allows you to connect the dots between your feelings and your actions.

A quick reminder: Don't let reflection turn into a cycle of self-blame. The past is behind you, and beating yourself up over it won't move you forward. Instead of focusing on the mistake, ask yourself what you can learn from it so you'd do better next time. We all mess up, and that's part of growing.

Reflection also means owning your reactions—taking responsibility for how you behave rather than blaming others or the situation.

We live in a world of finger-pointing, where responsibility has become a hot potato passed from hand to hand, person to person. "Well, I wouldn't have reacted that way if they hadn't said that." "The situation forced my hand." "I had no choice." Since when did your emotions and reactions belong to someone else's account ledger? Every burst of anger, every tear of frustration, every moment of despair—they're all yours, wholly and completely, to manage. No one can make you feel anything. The moment you blame someone else for your feelings is the moment you surrender your power to change them.

- **Write it down**

I know what you're thinking: *Seriously? Journaling? That's your big solution?*

Trust me, I had the same reaction. When someone first suggested I write down my feelings, I rolled my eyes so hard they practically got stuck. It seemed like something from an old movie, sitting there with a diary covered in hearts, writing "Dear Diary" and spilling all my secrets.

Hey, if that's your thing, I'm not judging! You do you. However, what I'm talking about is a lot less dramatic. No need for a fancy journal or perfect handwriting. Just a quick note in your phone, a notes app, or even a scrap of paper (but try not to lose it). The idea is to jot down three things: what happened, how your body felt, and what you did about it. For example, "Failed my history quiz. Chest felt tight, hands shaky. Told everyone to leave me alone at lunch." That's it.

But even those few sentences will tell you a lot about your patterns. You'll start to see how your body responds to certain triggers and how you handle them—giving you some serious insights into your emotional habits.

Fun Fact #13:

Your body releases stress hormones even for imagined scenarios. When you're overthinking something that hasn't even happened, your body still releases stress hormones as if it's real.

EMOTIONAL MODULATION: HOW TO STAY BALANCED

Once you're aware of what you're feeling, the next step is emotional modulation, which involves adjusting the intensity of your emotional response. This could mean using strategies, including the 90-second rule.

The physical response to an emotion—such as a racing heart, tight chest, or flushed face—actually only lasts about 90 seconds. According to Dr. Jill Bolte Taylor (2008), a neuroscientist, this brief physiological reaction occurs due to the brain triggering chemical and neural responses. After this 90-second window, the emotional response typically fades unless you continue to mentally re-trigger it by dwelling on the original thought.

So, what can you do during these 90 seconds to help yourself regulate and move on without escalating the emotion further? First, stop what you're doing, and then select one of these methods:

- **Count to 90 and chill:** Hit pause and count to 90 (in your head or out loud), but don't rush through it. Go slow, one number after another. Let your mind focus on each number, and feel as the stress fades away while your body chills out from the adrenaline blast.

- **Take a physical break:** Feeling fired up? If it's safe and appropriate, dip out of the situation for a bit. Your environment can add to the pressure; thus a quick walk or a brief change of scenery can help clear your head. For situations where leaving isn't an option, moving a little— something as simple as stretching or shaking out your arms and legs—will relieve some of that tension. It's your body's way of reducing the fight-or-flight response by burning off some of the excess adrenaline produced in moments of stress or anger.
- **Use visualization:** Close your eyes and visualize a peaceful, calming scene, such as a beach, forest, or any place where you feel relaxed. Imagine yourself fully immersed in that scene—hear the waves, feel the sun, or listen to the rustling leaves. Visualization shifts your brain's focus away from the trigger and creates a calming mental environment. This technique can be particularly effective for anxiety and fear-based emotions.
- **Focus on a simple distraction:** Manage to redirect your brain's attention to something else for a moment. Engage in a simple task that doesn't require much thought, like organizing your desk, listening to your favorite music, scrolling through calming photos, or doodling. Be sure it's a temporary distraction—you're not avoiding the issue; you're letting the initial surge of emotion pass before addressing the situation logically.
- **Let it out (safe physical release):** Forget what anyone's told you about "'keeping it together" or "staying balanced," even though you're feeling ready to explode. You need to let that pressure out—for real. Your body is built to express emotions so when those emotions get trapped inside, they start causing problems. From sleepless nights and anxiety

attacks to getting sick often and feeling physically drained, these are signs your body is struggling to release them. Get somewhere private—your bedroom, the shower, your car, or wherever you can be completely uninhibited. Then give yourself permission to be LOUD. Scream into your pillow until your throat hurts. Cry those ugly tears you've been holding back. Let out that guttural 'UGHHH' that's been sitting in your chest. Don't try to make it pretty—that's not the point. Go full volume, full emotion, full whatever-you're-feeling. After you're done, your body will naturally want to take some deep breaths. Let it. Let whatever's inside come out however it needs to.

Remember, not all situations need the same playbook. Cooling down anger is different from managing anxiety. Perfect control won't happen instantly, and emotional reactions may still slip through. But with time, you'll get much better at handling them, I promise.

Just don't wait for a full-on meltdown to try them out. If you're even slightly frustrated with homework or anything else, that's a great opportunity to practice the pause and breathing exercises. Every emotion, big or small, deserves a little love and attention!

Fun Fact #14:

Getting real about your emotions helps you accept yourself for real—and that's a mental health win.

EMOTIONAL RESPONSE: HANDLING THE AFTERMATH WITH PURPOSE

Alright, so you've done the work so far—you're aware of what's going on in your head and used some techniques to control it (which, by the way, happens in about 100 seconds), Now comes the last stage: How do you respond to all those emotions in healthy ways rather than on impulse or out of proportion to the situation?

As you may recall, I previously mentioned that emotional modulation is great for putting out fires in the moment, but it's not the permanent solution. To truly heal, you've got to face those emotional situations head-on. This is when you can choose to take positive action, whether it's addressing the issue directly or simply deciding to let go of the emotion and move on.

When you choose to express your emotions, even anger can be communicated productively if you do it right. Start by stating how you feel using "I" statements: *I feel frustrated when...* Avoid using lines like "You always make me angry," which puts the blame on the other person and invites defensiveness.

For important conversations, consider using the CLEAR method:

- **C**hoose your timing (when everyone is calm).
- **L**ead with how you feel.
- **E**xplain the specific situation (without blaming; focus on actions or events, not the person).
- **A**sk for what you need.
- **L**isten. **R**espect their response.

When Your Anger Isn't The Villain in Your Story and Nice Isn't Enough

Okay, pause the chill pill talk for a minute because if your siblings or best friend are being targeted by mean girls, the last thing you want to hear is about breathing calmly.

- **Ground your rage: You're in beast mode now—your heart's pounding, your hands are shaking, and that protec-**

tive fire is burning hot. But you'll need to calm down or you'll risk getting pulled into the fight. You want to be the person who stood up, not the one who lost control. Even if you "win" (whatever that means), you might end up with split knuckles, a suspension slip, or something worse. Plus, the moment it gets physical, you've handed the bully a gift-wrapped excuse to play victim.

• Find your power voice: Don't yell—that's amateur hour. Instead, drop your tone like you're laying down the law. "Stop. Now." Two words, but they hit strong when delivered right.

• Stand your ground: Plant your feet slightly apart, square your shoulders, and keep your chin level—not aggressive, but solid. Your body's sending a message before you even say "I'm not backing down."

• Choose your words: "That stops now." "Back off." "This isn't a discussion." "No. And I won't say it twice." Keep it short, firm, and final. No room for negotiation, no wasted breath.

• Know when to level up: If a situation feels unsafe or is escalating beyond your control, that's your cue to call in backup from someone who can help.

• The exit strategy: Once you've made your stand, have a plan to end the encounter on your terms. A simple "We're done here" and walking away can be more powerful than trying to have the last word. You've already said what you needed to say, so there's no point in continuing a conversation that's just going to go in circles. Be the one who knows their worth doesn't depend on winning a word war.

Not all emotional battles involve other people, though. The toughest fights usually happen inside your own head. That racing heart before a big test, the spiral of thoughts when you're lying in bed worrying about your future, or that overwhelming feeling when everything seems to pile up at once—those internal struggles need their own kind of response.

When you're dealing with internal pressure, the tricky part is that you're both the person feeling the emotion and the one who needs to handle it. There's no one else to talk it out (at least not immediately) and use those "I feel" statements with. You need strategies that work when you're alone with your thoughts. One of them is accepting what's happening in your body and mind. Your stress about the test is real. Those feelings of panic or overwhelm are real. Fighting them or telling yourself you shouldn't feel this way only adds another layer of stress. Instead, talk to yourself: *Okay, I'm feeling really stressed right now, and that's normal before a big test.*

Next, separate what you can control from what you can't. You can't change that the test is tomorrow. You can't make yourself a pro overnight. But you can control how you use the time you have right now. You can control your study environment. You can control when you decide to stop studying and get some rest. Are you putting too much pressure on yourself? Adjusting your expectations is also within your grasp.

Still, there are times when the smartest thing you can do with an emotion is...nothing at all. Not every emotion needs action. Let it pass through you like a bad song on the radio. No need to hit replay. To be clear, however, this isn't the same as suppressing emotions or pretending they don't exist. Rather, it's acknowledging the feeling but consciously deciding not to act on it. Maybe you totally lost it when your younger sibling borrowed your charger without asking. Yes, it's annoying, but does it deserve the level of rage you're feeling?

Reacting impulsively could make situations worse. You see your ex hanging out with someone new, and you want to post that embarrassing photo of them from last year. The satisfaction would last about two seconds, but the drama would go on forever. This is when release isn't a suggestion—it's a necessity.

Practice release when:

• the situation is already over and can't be changed.

• your emotional response is disproportionate to the trigger.

• acting on the emotion would cause more problems than it would solve.

• the issue isn't actually about you.

There are storms, and then there are hurricanes—the kind of life events that hit so hard, they make you constantly question yourself if things will ever feel normal again. Not the everyday ups and downs, but those moments that crack something deep inside you. Maybe you've lived through something that's changed how you see the world—your parents splitting up, moving to a place where everything feels foreign, or discovering truths about yourself that both terrify and liberate you. Or perhaps you've lost someone who was your anchor—the person who made Monday mornings bearable with their stupid jokes or who knew exactly what to say when nothing felt right.

I hesitate to bring this up because I never want to sound alarming or add to your worries, but it needs to be said that unhealed emotional wounds don't stay in your heart alone—they seep into your whole body. I've seen it happen—people carrying grief or trauma for years until their bodies start sending urgent messages through physical symptoms, such as tumors, heart disease, or cancer.

Even the mightiest figures in Greek mythology, if they were walking among us today, wouldn't be immune to their emotions. They would all be vulnerable to the reality that unhealed emotional wounds find ways to make themselves heard. So I'm asking you, with all the care in my heart, to be gentler with yourself than those figures were. Take action before your body sends out a signal that's too late to ignore.

If you broke your leg, nobody would tell you to walk it off or do some breathing exercises. They'd get you to a doctor. Your emotional wounds deserve the same level of care. So, let's be real; are you struggling to fall asleep even when you're wiped out? Or do you sleep for hours but still feel drained? If so, don't wait—seek help IMMEDIATELY. This isn't something you should try to figure out alone. Find a trusted adult—a parent, teacher, or school counselor—and let them know what's going on.

Your parents or guardians might not always understand what you're going through right away, but they need to know when you're struggling with something serious. They can connect you with a therapist or counselor who specializes in working with teenagers. If talking face-to-face feels too overwhelming at first, there are other ways to reach out. Many schools now have anonymous reporting systems where you can request to talk to a counselor. Text-based crisis lines specifically for teenagers, where you can start the conversation through messages instead of having to speak out loud, are also available.

Key Takeaways:

• **Your emotions can talk, but you don't have to take orders. You're the boss, not them.**

• Snapping at people feels powerful for two seconds, then awkward forever. Find a better outlet.

• If you wouldn't describe your entire life in one word, don't do it to your emotions. Be specific.

• Feelings hit hard, but if you don't fuel them, they fade in 90 seconds.

• Your feelings, your responsibility.

• Not every emotion needs a grand finale. Some are better off slipping away unnoticed.

• Ignoring stress and emotions? They'll show up as exhaustion, stomachaches, or random mood swings later.

7
LACK OF ROLE MODELS AND THE INFLUENCE OF FALSE IDOLS

Every morning, millions of teen girls around the world wake up and, before even getting out of bed, scroll through meticulously curated highlight reels of other people's lives. By the time they brush their teeth, they've already absorbed hundreds of messages about who they should be, what success means, and how far they fall short of both. But what if what looks like gold turns out to be carefully painted brass?

They're everywhere you look—the so-called role models—with their perfectly presented lives, flawless skin, and seemingly effortless success stories flooding your screen every time you scroll. Are they really all they seem? Or are they really, really good at tricking you into thinking they have it all together? What's behind those Instagram stories? We see the perfect shots, the "spontaneous" beach photos, but have you ever wondered what happens when the camera's off? Do these "role models" have bad hair days? Do they drop their phones in the toilet, like the rest of us? Above all, do they leave you feeling inspired or in a quick moment of awe that disappears as soon as the screen goes dark?

Back in the day, our grandmothers' role models were people they could actually watch in action—people who lived their lives in the public eye, showing their triumphs, their struggles, and everything in between. Now? We're swimming in a sea of highlight reels, and the crazy part is, it's not even us picking our role models anymore. They're chosen for us by algorithms that know exactly how to keep us hooked while our own real growth and well-being get lost in the process or replaced by endless comparisons.

As we move through this chapter, you'll discover how your brain processes role models, why false idols are so magnetically attractive, and how to create your own "influence immunity"—a mental skill that lets you absorb the good stuff while filtering out the noise.

More than that, we're going to challenge some pretty fundamental assumptions about what it means to look up to someone in the first place. After all, the most powerful role models aren't the ones who make you want to be them; they're those who make you want to be a better version of yourself.

The "Us vs. Them" Game

Social media thrives on division. The more divided we are, the more engaged we become. For this reason, content often frames issues in extreme ways because it's easier to control people when they pick a side.

In fact, debates online aren't really about understanding. They're about proving your side is right and the other side is wrong. That's intentional. Platforms don't want discussion; they want conflict. Conflict fuels engagement; engagement fuels profit.

The False Idols

Influencers operate as brands, marketing tools, and money-making machines. Many don't even believe themselves in what they promote —they simply know what gets people to buy.

Idolizing them gives them the power to shape your beliefs, your desires, and even your reality. And most of the time, they're just performing—playing a persona, a character thoughtfully designed to keep you invested.

COMMON MANIPULATION TACTICS USED TO CREATE FALSE NARRATIVES

Social media doesn't simply share information; it shapes, twists, bends, and serves it back to you in a way that convinces you the conclusion was yours all along. But was it?

Have you ever questioned why certain posts made you angry? Why others made you believe your life wasn't enough? Why some content made you side with people you barely know, fighting against others you've never even met? That's not an accident. That's design—an entire ecosystem built to control the way you think, feel, and react. And the scariest part? It works.

The Illusion of Choice

You open your favorite app and start scrolling. Hundreds of posts. Different opinions. A variety of "news" sources. It gives the impression that you have access to all perspectives, doesn't it? However, what you see is heavily filtered. Algorithms decide which posts to show you, and they're based on what they want you to engage with. Not what's true. Not what's balanced. Just what keeps you hooked.

It's called the filter bubble—a term that describes the way social media personalizes your content to reinforce what you already believe. The more you like or engage with certain types of content, the more you get trapped in that digital echo chamber.

The Outrage Machine

The posts with the most comments and shares are usually the most controversial. That's because outrage is one of the easiest ways to get people to engage as it travels faster than happiness. Drama keeps people glued to the screen. The more heated you get, the longer you'll stick around. And guess who profits from that? Definitely not you.

It's why headlines are designed to trigger a reaction. Why posts exaggerate. Why misinformation spreads like wildfire. People don't always fact-check when they're emotional. They just react. And social media companies love that.

Manufactured Perfection

Scroll long enough, and perfection is everywhere—effortless beauty, golden-hour selfies, morning rituals that belong in a magazine. Meanwhile, you tell yourself you're the one who's falling short.

That's a manipulation tactic.

Because the more insecure you feel, the more you'll immerse yourself with content that promises to "fix" you. More beauty products. More self-improvement hacks. More ways to "glow up." It's a cycle designed to keep you feeling almost happy, but never quite there.

The Viral Lie

A lie doesn't have to be true to go viral. It only has to be believable enough and emotionally triggering. A strategically cropped image, a misrepresented quote, or a minor exaggeration can be enough to mislead. And once it spreads, it becomes accepted as fact. Even when corrected, the damage is irreversible. The truth struggles to reach those who already believed the lie.

Fun Fact #15:

Science says getting "likes" on your posts lights up your brain as though you just won the lottery—or got the last slice of pizza. Blame it on the nucleus accumbens, the

brain's little hype man for rewards and pleasure (Sherman et al., 2016).

PSYCHOLOGY OF FALSE IDOLS: WHY ARE WE DRAWN TO THEM?

We tend to admire those who have qualities we wish we had. We look at their beauty, wealth, success, and lifestyle and think, *I want that. I could be that.* This is normal because it's how many of us would measure our own success and self-worth. In the age of social media, however, we're not admiring from a distance—we're actively involved in forming relationships with these figures in relationships that are, in fact, entirely one-sided. We form connections with media personalities who don't even know we exist.

Simply put, the constant exposure we get through platforms like Instagram, YouTube, and TikTok creates a false sense of intimacy. We feel like we "know" these influencers or celebrities, and they know us, but this is far from reality.

Why does this happen? Why are we so drawn to these one-sided relationships?

Social media has created a breeding ground for these *parasocial* bonds to grow. Platforms like Instagram and YouTube allow influencers to present themselves in an almost intimate way, sharing snippets of their personal lives. You get to see them wake up, work out, eat breakfast, and chat with their followers. You participate through likes, comments, and shares, and in return, you get a tiny bit of their life, often curated to perfection. It feels personal and real, even though it's only a performance. This level of exposure is something we've never had before. Gradually you start feeling a connection, an emotional bond. You even think of them as your "friends," "confidants," or "role models."

This leads to a self-perpetuating cycle where each interaction deepens the perceived intimacy. Every morning check-in, every comment left and every story watched strengthens these invisible ties. The dopamine hits from these interactions, combined with the comfort these "friendships" provide, create bonds that feel too precious to break.

Perhaps most significantly, these *parasocial* relationships offer something uniquely appealing in our increasingly isolated modern world: connection without vulnerability. We can feel close to someone without risking rejection, share in their triumphs without exposing our own failures, and experience intimacy without the messiness of real human interaction. This safety, however artificial, makes these bonds particularly difficult to relinquish, no matter whether we recognize their one-sided nature or not.

Going back to my earlier point, this connection is illusory; we don't actually know these people. What we know is what they choose to show us—filtered, edited, and polished. They show us highlight reels featuring the perfect version of their lives. As a result, we're left with two reactions: idealizing an illusion or resenting the gap between our lives and theirs.

Fun Fact #16:

TikTok's algorithm can figure out your interests within 10 minutes of use, tracking how long you pause on a video rather than just your likes.

The Internalization of False Ideals

When we see someone gain success, wealth, or beauty without much effort, we start to believe that's how it works for everyone. *Oh, so that's how it works. Just blink twice, and boom—rich, famous, flawless.*

We somewhat internalize the idea that success comes quickly and easily, that it's a straight shot to fame or fortune. If that's true, then why the need to push? Why put in effort when the outcome is already set in stone? And with that thought alone, we slow down. Instead of inspiring action, these glimpses of "effortless" success breed inertia. Meanwhile, success doesn't knock. It doesn't send a calendar invite, and by the time we realize we were supposed to chase it, the game is already over.

There's also the other side of this—seeing success happen overnight, again and again, messing with our heads. It tricks us into thinking that effort isn't what gets you there—luck is. Consequently, we stop believing effort actually matters. If success is all about luck or some magic "it factor," then what's the point of trying?

The irony is that the more we scroll through stories of people making it in life with ease, the less we believe in our own chances. Success then feels out of reach—not because it really is, but because we're too afraid to be the only ones struggling while everyone else seems to just be gliding through to the top. So we give up. We wait for our lucky break, wait for things to magically click. And in that waiting, we lose the very thing that could've gotten us there in the first place —trying.

The Comparison Curse

False idols aren't limited to celebrities, influencers, and the people with millions of followers. They're anyone who seems to embody the "ideal" version of who you wish you could be. The girl with the effortless beauty, the guy with the million-dollar business, the influencer who seems to always be on vacation, glowing and unbothered. They don't just have what you want; they are what you want to be.

We admire individuals who have what we value, and when someone seems to have all of those things at once, admiration turns into something stronger—maybe even something close to worship.

There's nothing wrong with that. But what happens when you admire someone so much that it makes you feel worse about yourself? What happens when their perfection makes you hyper-aware of everything you're not?

This is where admiration gets tangled up with envy. Because these idols don't merely represent success; they represent your own perceived failure. Every time you compare yourself to them, the gap between where you are and where they are feels impossible to close. Their life becomes a constant reminder of what you don't have and what you're not. Then, admiration stops being inspiring. Instead of lifting you up, it pulls you under.

Envy doesn't announce itself and show up as *I hate them*. It sneaks in as something smaller. "Wow, she's so lucky." "Must be nice to have everything handed to you." "If I had their life, I'd be happy too." And in the past, admiration had distance. You saw a celebrity in a magazine and watched an actress in a movie, and that was it. Today, they live in your phone, which means the envy will never go away. Every time you turn on your gadgets, it's there waiting for you.

The problem with envy isn't only that it makes you feel bad; it rewires how you see yourself. The more you compare, the more you start believing that success, beauty, happiness—those things belong to them, not to you. It fuels your desire for more while making you believe you are less. Less beautiful. Less successful. Less worthy.

Right after you fall into this admiration-envy trap, you slip into the why-even-try mindset. Why bother when you'll never be that girl, that guy, that person? False idols steal your drive, and so, you just stop.

BUILDING YOUR "INFLUENCE IMMUNITY"

You get 86,400 seconds a day. Scrolling eats them up fast. But what you're really losing isn't just time but a clear view of yourself. Every video, every image, and every story builds a wall between you and your real life.

To break this wall, start practicing conscious digital consumption. *What am I really seeking here? What am I trading for this moment of digital stimulation?* Awareness is your first line of defense against digital manipulation. Be intentional. Question what you see. If an influencer claims something "changed their life overnight," ask for the control group. Where's the peer review? What's the methodology behind their "miracle morning routine"?

Choose content you consume instead of letting the algorithm decide. Scroll with awareness and limit passive scrolling. Obviously, there's a huge difference between using social media and letting social media use you.

More than that, you have to decide how you react to someone's perfect vacation photos. Examine whether that "a day in the life" of a successful entrepreneur makes you doubt your own path or serves as a source of motivation. Appreciate without attaching your worth to what you see. Take everything as inspiration—no less, no more—to free yourself from the weight of comparison and open your eyes to what's possible for you, in your own way, at your own time.

Along the way, don't forget to look up and pay attention to the world happening right in front of you. The people who can inspire you are usually the ones whose lives you get to witness firsthand. They don't need to be famous. They don't need a Wikipedia page or a million followers. They just need to be real, present, and living authentically.

Make no mistake—I'm not implying that icons like Clara Barton, Marie Curie, Mother Teresa, or any other honored historical figures aren't worth your admiration. No, not at all. Their accomplishments, their brilliance, their resilience—they can inspire us in immeasurable ways. They've paved the way for many of us to dream bigger, reach higher, and challenge the impossible. But imagine what it would be like to meet them in person—to hear their voices, watch them work, see their struggles, and learn from them directly. That kind of inspiration is unforgettable.

So, who are these people, you ask? They could be the teacher who stays after class to make sure you understand, the friend who reminds you of your worth when you doubt yourself, or the mentor who leads by example rather than words. They could be the grandmother who's raising a family with nothing but determination and love. They could be a friend who refuses to give up on their dreams, no matter how many times they fall. They could even be a stranger who offers a hand when they have nothing to gain. You don't need to look far to find inspiration. Sometimes, all it takes is looking around.

It's one thing to know about perseverance through historical accounts or viral clips; it's another to see someone in your life embody it. It's one thing to hear about innovation in the abstract or through perfectly edited content; it's another to watch someone push boundaries and adapt to challenges right in front of you. There's a reason why hands-on learning is more effective than passive observation. The same applies to inspiration—what is real and within reach will always leave a deeper impression than what is distant and idealized.

But be mindful of where you look for it. If you only draw inspiration from those who look like you, think like you, and live like you, you limit yourself to a narrow version of success, resilience, and wisdom. Strength has many forms. Determination doesn't always look the same. Success isn't defined by one single narrative.

A scientist's persistence in the lab can teach you about patience as much as an artist's relentless pursuit of creativity. A single mother working two jobs can show you resilience as powerfully as a world-class athlete training for the Olympics. A refugee rebuilding their life in a new country can redefine your understanding of courage as much as a CEO leading a billion-dollar company.

Every background, every struggle, every journey carries something worth learning. As such, expanding the range of voices we listen to significantly matters. The more perspectives we embrace, the richer and more well-rounded our own understanding of perseverance, innovation, and success becomes.

Fun Fact #18:

Studies show that even brief exposure to ultra-curated beauty images can lower self-esteem, even when people know the images are edited (Booth, 2024).

Practical Exercises and Activities

The following exercises will guide you in assessing your role models, filtering your sources of inspiration, and taking proactive steps toward becoming the person you aspire to be.

1. Social Media Audit Guide

Take charge of your digital environment. A social media audit helps you filter out content that hinders your growth and ensures that what you engage with aligns with your values and reality.

Instructions:

- Scroll through your feed and identify 5-10 accounts you engage with the most.
- For each, ask:
  - Does this account educate, uplift, or inspire me?
  - Does it make me feel inadequate or pressure me into comparison?
  - Am I following out of habit, or is this adding real value to my life?
- Unfollow or mute any account that negatively impacts your mindset.
- Follow at least three new accounts that align with your values, growth, and aspirations.

2. Mentor Outreach Templates

Finding the right words when reaching out to a mentor isn't always easy. You can use these templates as a foundation for crafting personalized messages when seeking guidance from potential mentors.

Template 1: Formal Request

Subject: Seeking Guidance & Mentorship Opportunity

Dear [Mentor's Name],

I admire your work in [specific field or achievement] and the impact you've had in [relevant industry/community]. As someone striving to grow in [your goal/area of interest], I would love the opportunity to learn from your insights and experiences.

If you're open to it, I would greatly appreciate a short conversation to discuss your journey and any advice you may have for someone in my position. I understand your time is valuable and would be grateful for any guidance you're willing to share.

Looking forward to the possibility of connecting. Thank you for your time!

Best,

[Your Name]

Template 2: Casual Approach

Hey [Mentor's Name],

I've been following your work in [specific field] and really admire how you [mention something specific about their work]. I'm currently working on [your goal/interest] and would love to hear your thoughts on how to proceed.

Would you be open to a quick chat sometime? No pressure—just really inspired by what you do and would appreciate any insights!

Thanks so much!

3. Role Model Evaluation Worksheet

Who you admire says a lot about who you aspire to be. Whether your role models influence you through their persistence, originality, leadership, or self-discipline, this worksheet will help you break down their qualities and apply them to your own life.

Instructions: List three people you consider as your role models (they can be historical figures, public figures, or individuals in your personal life). For each, identify

- the qualities you admire most.
- a specific action or achievement that made them stand out to you.

- how their values align with yours.
- a way you can apply their lessons in your life

<u>Reflect</u>: Are your role models shaping your mindset in a way that supports your goals? If not, who else could you learn from?

<u>Key Takeaways</u>:

- **Influencers are just people with good Wi-Fi. Don't let their "perfect" look fool you. They've got struggles, too—probably involving spilled coffee or Wi-Fi drama.**

- **Your brain craves drama—unfortunately. Social media is a master at triggering your emotions. It probably knows you a lot better than your BFF.**

- **You don't need a filter to be fabulous. Stop comparing your unfiltered self to someone else's highlight reel.**

- **Your time on social media is yours. Don't waste it letting someone else's life mess with your head.**

- **Don't let algorithms be your life coach. TikTok may know your likes, but only you know what makes you happy. Go find that!**

8

ENVISIONING YOUR FUTURE AND EXPLORING CAREER OPTIONS

One way or another, invisible hands are sketching the outline of who you might become. Social media algorithms whisper about dream careers. Family traditions paint pictures of acceptable paths. Society's expectations draw boundaries around your ambitions. Your true dreams, though, are off in the corner, waiting for a chance to be heard.

Career guides tell you to "follow your passion," but last time I checked, passion isn't a GPS coordinate you could plug into Google Maps. They say "do what you love," but forget to mention that love is complex, changing, and often needs to be discovered through experience rather than intuition. They promise that if you check all the right boxes—good grades, right college, perfect internships—success will follow like night follows day.

They've given their advice, but no one's explaining that the future of work will most probably look nothing like its past. The careers that will define your generation may not be existing yet. The skills that will matter most, in all likelihood, haven't been named. The problems you'll solve are still to emerge. The tools you'll use are yet to be invented. Think about how just 10 years ago, the idea of AI running half the world was something you'd only see in a dystopian movie, where robots take over and humans are stuck fighting for survival. Now, AI is in your phone, your car, and probably even your fridge, and who knows? In the next decade, it could even be in your body. You're not simply choosing a career—you're stepping into a revolution, and as part of the Alpha generation, you've got the first-row seat to all the chaos and excitement.

We're standing at a crossroads of human history where the success rules are getting rewritten as we speak. The stable careers our parents knew are starting to dissolve. The clear paths are becoming overgrown with new possibilities. The skills that guaranteed success yesterday might be obsolete tomorrow. So, forget the question "What do you want to be when you grow up?" That's a relic from a time when careers were linear and lifelong. The real question now is, "What problems do you want to solve? What changes do you want to create? How do you want the world to remember you?" These questions don't have right or wrong answers, but they do have consequences. Your responses will shape not just your career, but the future itself.

TODAY'S YOU VS. FUTURE YOU

Right now, there are two versions of you living rent-free in your mind: the person you are today and the person you imagine becoming. Funny enough, these two versions are living in completely different universes.

"Today's you" might be struggling with calculus while "future you" is somehow running a tech startup. "Today's you" gets nervous speaking in front of the class, but "future You" is giving TED talks. "Today's you" can barely decide what to wear to school, while "future you" has it all figured out—the dream job, the perfect life, the whole package.

"Future you" is both closer and farther than you think. Closer because every single choice you make today is already molding who you'll become. Farther, because transformation isn't about dramatic overnight changes—it's about small decisions compounding over time.

Want to be a successful entrepreneur? "Today's you" needs to start developing business acumen, even if it's through running a small online shop. Dream of being a renowned artist? "Today's you" should be sketching daily, even if the results aren't yet Instagram-worthy. Aspire to lead a tech company? "Today's you" must start understanding technology trends, even if coding intimidates you.

In other words, "future you" isn't some stranger waiting at the finish line of your teens. It's being built right now, choice by choice, habit by habit, decision by decision. Every time you push through something difficult, try something new, and choose growth over comfort —you're doing more than helping "today's you;" you're literally creating "future you."

So, stop waiting for that "right" moment. It's not coming in three years. It's not coming in five years. It's not coming when you graduate. Every second you spend waiting for the "right time" is a second lost. Your skills, knowledge, and experiences—they're all seeds that need time to grow. You can't plant them the day you need them and expect immediate results. They require months, years even, to develop into something substantial. The changes you want to see in your life should begin today, because life doesn't hit pause for you to catch up. It moves forward every second, and with each passing moment, "future you" is becoming a little more real.

Fun Fact #19:

90% of the world's data was created in the last two years! We are generating more information than ever before, and

the skills to analyze, filter, and apply knowledge will be more valuable than memorizing facts (SINTEF, 2013).

WHY MOST FUTURE PLANS FAIL (AND HOW TO AVOID THAT)

Most career plans look great on paper. The steps are clear, the goals are set, and the timeline seems perfect. But when these plans hit reality, they often crumble. No, not because fate's out to get you or you're slacking off.

The main reason career plans fail is the belief in a "perfect path." You know the one—get good grades, pick the right college major, land the ideal internship, and *voilà!*, your dream career materializes like magic. This thinking is dangerous because it

- makes you ignore valuable opportunities that don't fit the "perfect" plan.
- creates unnecessary stress when things don't go exactly as planned.
- blinds you to new possibilities that might even be better than your original goal.

How many successful people are doing exactly what they planned when they were in school? Probably only a few, I'd guess. Most game-changing innovations came from people who went "off script" and found unexpected connections between different fields and experiences. J.K. Rowling was a single mom on welfare before she wrote Harry Potter. Sara Blakely started out selling fax machines and then went on to invent Spanx. Beyoncé began her career in a girl group, but now she's not just an award-winning artist; she's a brand, a mogul, and an icon. Plans? Nah—they created legacies instead!

This goes to show that the road to success isn't always a straight line, and it rarely follows the script we write in our heads. Embrace the mess. Accept that your journey will take unexpected turns. View detours as learning opportunities. Understand that "failures" can redirect you to better things.

Keep your goals clear and your methods flexible. If your path doesn't look like what you imagined, that's okay. Focus on where you want to go, but be open to how you get there. Success doesn't always come in the way you expect, but if you're adaptable, you'll be ready to seize it when it does.

Another common trap is planning your career around today's in-demand skills. Sure, coding bootcamps might be hot right now, but what about five years from now? Ten years? The skills that guarantee employment today might be completely replaced by automation tomorrow. So, don't make the mistake of

- learning only what's required for your target job.
- focusing on technical know-how while ignoring adaptable skills.
- following current trends without considering future developments.

At the same time, you'll want to build a foundation of adaptable abilities that will matter regardless of how the job market changes. These include the following abilities:

- learning how to learn
- problem-solving methods
- communication skills
- critical thinking
- emotional intelligence

These skills remain valuable even as specific technical requirements evolve.

Also, steer clear of planning your future based on others' expectations, chasing prestige over passion, prioritizing family approval over your own dreams, or measuring success by salary and title rather than personal fulfillment. This mindset fails because it

- leads to burnout (trying to live up to others' expectations is exhausting).
- ignores your natural strengths and interests.
- fosters an endless craving for outside validation.
- causes you to overlook opportunities that could align better with who you are.

Last but not least, follow your interests and curiosity over trends. Your "weird" interests are not odd at all, and there is absolutely nothing wrong with you if you're not jumping on the trending bandwagon. Nobody ever changed the world by being a knockoff version of someone else. Ada Lovelace didn't pioneer computer programming because it was a hot career skill (in 1843, computers didn't even exist)—she was driven by an unrelenting curiosity about how machines could be used to solve complex problems. Katherine Johnson didn't help NASA with complex calculations because space was the hot field—she was determined to use her math skills to ensure that humans could explore the stars. Hedy Lamarr didn't invent a frequency-hopping technique because it was trending—she was motivated by a desire to solve problems and contribute to wartime efforts, leading to technology used in modern communication systems.

The future doesn't belong to the people who can follow instructions best (we have AI for that now, thanks). By the time something becomes a trend, you're already late to the party. Yesterday it was crypto trading. Today it's learning to code. Tomorrow it'll probably be quantum brain surgery or whatever trend decides to take over our feeds. The trends will constantly change. Still, the real opportunities are always in such weird stuff that makes you lose track of time—the stuff that makes your friends say, "Why are you so obsessed with that?" Only with genuine curiosity can you learn at lightning speed, think on a deeper level, and come up with ideas that someone too focused on trends could never dream of.

WHERE IT ALL BEGINS: UNDERSTANDING YOUR STARTING POINT

The hardest part of starting isn't the starting—it's figuring out what it is you're actually starting with.

Right now, you're sitting on a collection of abilities, experiences, and possibilities that you've probably never fully cataloged. How funny it is that most of us are hilariously bad at seeing ourselves clearly—we notice our flaws in HD and our strengths in low resolution.

For a solid future plan, you need to get real about where you are. Not where you think you should be, not where others expect you to be, but where you actually are. You can't build anything without a foundation, right? Get clear on where you're at, or everything you try to do will be a waste of time.

Start with the stuff you know for sure—your *skills*. Not only the ones you'd put on a resume, but all of them. These can be anything from academic abilities to tech skills like coding, social media management, and design. What skills do you use most often? What do people turn to you for help with? These skills form the building blocks for where you'll go next.

Then, there are the stuff that make you stand out—your *strengths*. But they're not what you're good at; they're the things you can't help but do. They're the lens through which you see the world. They're the tools you naturally reach for when solving problems. Above all, they're what energizes you. You might be capable at math but find it draining. That's a skill, not a strength. A strength is something that, even when hard, gives you energy.

Sometimes, it's only when we try something new that we realize what we're truly capable of. Stepping out of your comfort zone and trying different things can reveal hidden talents. This is where you can be bold and experimental. If you're unsure where to begin, think about the things that intrigue you but you've never tried pursuing. Maybe you've always wanted to get into photography but haven't had the courage to take it up. Or perhaps you've been curious about coding, graphic design, or volunteering but never made the time to explore them. These new experiences can help you discover abilities you never knew you had and push you to uncover more of what you're capable of.

And don't forget your *passions*. They're your "true north"—the motivating force behind everything you do. They're the reasons you wake up every day and push through obstacles. Look at your daily life. What do you spend most of your time doing? Pay attention to what you naturally gravitate toward. Is it drawing, singing, or helping friends with their problems? Do you lose track of time when you're playing a sport or dancing to music? These everyday habits hold the clues to your passion.

If you're constantly doodling in the margins of your notebooks, creating playlists, or trying out new makeup techniques, it's likely that creativity is a big part of your life. If you're always fixing things around the house, solving problems, or figuring out how to optimize your study routine, your passion might lean more toward logic, problem-solving, or organization.

The *tools* you have (or don't have) at your disposal play a huge role in the journey ahead too. They tell you to "pursue your passions," to "follow your dream," but they forget to mention the equipment, resources, and access you'll need. At this moment, you might be sitting in a room dreaming big but feeling stuck because you don't have what you need. Maybe it's tech that's out of reach. Or software that costs more than your monthly allowance. Or connections to people who could open doors for you. You can see where you want to go, but the bridge to get there seems missing.

This is where most people stop. They look at what they're missing and decide they can't start until they have everything they need. But that's backwards thinking. Actually, you don't need all of them to start—you just need enough to take the first step.

No music studio? Start with your phone's voice recorder and free audio software. Learn about sound design using whatever you can access. Study mixing techniques with free online stems. The constraints will force you to be more creative with less.

Can't afford expensive courses? There are probably free alternatives. Maybe not as polished, and comprehensive, but enough to start learning. Mix YouTube tutorials, free online resources, and practical experimentation.

Lacking a professional network? Build one from scratch. Join online communities. Contribute to discussions. Share what you learn. When you start from nothing, every connection you make is intentional and meaningful.

No quiet space to work? Libraries exist. Community centers exist. School classrooms after hours exist. And if none of those work, there are always those early mornings or late nights when the world gets quieter. It's not ideal, but it's not impossible either.

Figure out which tools are absolutely essential for your next step. Make the most of what you have while working toward what you need. Start saving or planning for what will level up your work. Every successful person started somewhere, usually with less than they wanted.

THREE YEARS FROM NOW

The problem with most future plans is that they are stuck in a hazy "someday" that never arrives. "Someday I'll start my own company," "Someday I'll learn to dance," "Someday I'll create something amazing." But someday isn't a plan. It's an excuse to avoid starting now.

Your brain knows the difference between "someday" and "by 2029." Someday lets you off the hook. It doesn't demand anything from you right now. But 2029? That's real. That's countable. That's a deadline your brain takes seriously.

But why three years? That's because three years is enough time to become someone completely different, but not so long that you can't imagine it. You can learn an entirely new skill set. Master a craft. Build something from nothing. Start and grow a business. Three years gives you enough time to get seriously good at something without losing focus or getting lost in far-future fantasies. It's the time frame where you have the most control. You're old enough to make real decisions but young enough that you haven't locked yourself into major commitments. These years are yours to design.

Making Your Three-Year Goal Work

Get specific about where you want to be in three years. Not "be good at digital art" but "have a portfolio of 20 commissioned pieces and regular paying clients." Not "learn to code" but "build five working apps and land a junior developer position."

In three years, of course, you won't become a billionaire CEO. You won't become a world-famous astronaut. You won't master every skill that interests you. But you can turn zero coding knowledge into solid programming skills, transform a basic art hobby into a small freelance business, build a social media following from 0 to 10,000 engaged followers, or learn a new language to conversation level. Big dreams are great, but they have to be realistic and attainable within a specific time frame. Three years is enough time to build something real, but only if you're honest about what "real" means. After all, achieving 80% of a realistic goal beats achieving 0% of an impossible one.

You also need ways to know if you're actually moving forward. Numbers work best as in the following cases:

- How many pieces have you created?
- What specific skills have you mastered?
- How many people have you connected with?
- What concrete results can you show?

Numbers don't lie. Keeping track proves you're making progress. Otherwise, you might trick yourself into thinking you're growing when you're really just staying busy. Plus, measuring progress helps you separate what's working, what's not, and what needs adjusting. Progress becomes intentional, and that's how you make the next three years count.

Remember:

- **Progress isn't always visible day to day.**

- **Small steps count if they're in the right direction.**

- **Consistency beats intensity.**

- **Done is better than perfect.**

THE PROJECT TRIANGLE: YOU CAN'T HAVE IT ALL— SO PICK YOUR PRIORITIES

Whatever career you pick, it comes with trade-offs between three key things: time, money, and quality of life. These factors are interconnected, and you can't always maximize all three at once.

Want to become a doctor? You'll make great money and have high job satisfaction, but you'll trade away your time for years of intense study and demanding work hours. Dream of being a successful entrepreneur? You might get time flexibility and high earning potential, but you'll sacrifice stability and predictable income, especially in the early years. Love the idea of being a digital nomad? You'll get freedom with your time and potentially good quality of life, but you might need to accept lower or unpredictable income.

No path is perfect—only the one where you're aware of its trade-offs, shake hands with them, and accept them as part of the deal. Don't try finding a way out of making sacrifices because it's selecting the sacrifices that won't have you standing in the shower every morning questioning your life choices. Don't choose based on what sounds glamorous; pick based on what won't have you sending "I need to quit" texts to your friends every other week. I'd hate to see you years from now, dramatically staring out the window while spiraling into regret and blaming me for not warning you.

VISION BOARD: PINTEREST FOR YOUR FUTURE (BUT MAKE IT REAL)

A vision board is more than a bunch of pictures glued onto a poster. It's your brain's search engine for opportunities and a visual reminder of your goals, passions, and the future you're building. When you get clear about what you want, your brain starts noticing things it would've otherwise just scrolled right past before. It's like when you learn a new word, and all of a sudden, you hear it everywhere. Or when you start thinking about getting a certain type of car, and unexpectedly, you spot that model on every street corner. This way, you don't just think about your goals—you feel them. You feel excited, driven, and inspired to take action.

Crafting a vision board is pretty simple. You grab some clip art books (or Google images), scissors, and glue, and start finding pictures, words, and phrases that inspire you. These images should represent your goals, your passions, and your dream life. Want to travel the world? Find pictures of exotic places. Dream of becoming a tech genius? Find a pic of someone coding or a shiny new computer. The idea is to fill your board with things that represent your vision of the future. With a vision board that really speaks to you every time you look at it, you're reminded of the bigger picture. It becomes a source of motivation and focus, especially when the grind gets tough and distractions start to pull you in every direction.

In case it wasn't clear, a vision board isn't about *wishing* for things to happen but *claiming* them. Let's gaze at your dream house, fancy car, or luxury vacation, and hear yourself say, *This belongs to me. I'm making it happen.*

Steps to Create Your Vision Board

1. **Get clear on your goals:** Before you start cutting out random pictures, take a second to think about what you

truly want in your life. It could be a career, lifestyle, relationship, health, or something specific like launching a YouTube channel or traveling to 10 countries. Know exactly what you're working toward.

2. **Gather materials:** No need to go overboard with fancy supplies. A simple poster board, scissors, glue, and some clip art books (or printouts from the internet) will do the trick. If you prefer to keep things digital, no worries—apps like Canva are perfect for creating a sleek, online version of your vision board.

3. **Find images and words:** Start hunting for images that make you feel something deep inside. Whether it's a photo of a destination you've always wanted to visit, a quote that pushes you to be your best, or a picture of someone who inspires you to live the life you want, make sure everything you choose speaks to your heart. This is your vision board— let it be filled with the things that resonate with your dreams and ambitions. If it excites you, it belongs on your board.

4. **Arrange and glue:** With your images in hand, start laying them out on your board. There's no rush—take your time to arrange and rearrange until the pieces feel like they belong together. Go with what your heart tells you. Don't stress about making it look perfect—this is your personal vision board, and it's all about what strikes a chord with you. Once everything feels right, glue it down and let the vision unfold.

5. **Place it somewhere visible:** The whole point of a vision board is that it's something you see every day. Put it somewhere you'll notice easily—on your wall, next to your desk, or even above your bed. Make it a daily habit to look at it and ask yourself, *What's one thing I can do today to get closer to this vision?* The more often you do this, the more it sharpens your growth mindset.

Your vision board is your permission slip to want what you want, to dream what you dream, and to value what you value. Use it as a reminder that your path doesn't have to look like anyone else's to be valid and valuable. And most importantly, have fun with it. Your future isn't a test you have to pass; it's a story you get to write yourself. Make it a good one.

Key Takeaways:

• **Who you become isn't decided by one big moment—it's the little things you do daily (yes, even the boring stuff).**

• **If you're forcing yourself to like something because it looks good on paper, you're already losing.**

• **Being "good" at something doesn't mean you love it.**

• **People built empires with way less than what you have in your pocket right now.**

• **The version of you three years from now will probably laugh at what you think you want today.**

• **You don't need all the answers to build your future. You just need to start. Now, go!**

YOUR 30-DAY GLOW-UP CHALLENGE

Attention everybody!!!

Your current operating system is going to have an update. Ready to download "Version 2.0 of yourself?"

What's new in this version:

- enhanced mood management features
- updated self-talk software
- advanced energy tracking capabilities
- premium anti-doubt security system
- new and improved confidence boosters

What you'll need:

- a journal (digital or paper—your choice!)
- your favorite pens or markers
- a phone or device for tracking
- 15-20 minutes each day for the activities
- an open mind and a kind heart (especially toward yourself!)

But before you begin:

Quick journal prompt:

Why did you choose to start this challenge? Write a letter to your future self about what you hope to discover or achieve.

Week 1: Foundation Building: Self-Awareness and Understanding

Before we get into your big dreams and life goals, let's start with the foundation—understanding yourself.

Day 1: Getting to Know Your Cycle

- Start tracking your energy levels and mood.
- Learn how hormones affect your brain and performance.

Pro tips:

- Download a cycle tracking app (I recommend CycleSync or Flo).
- Rate your energy levels (1-10).
- Note your mood using emojis.
- Record any physical sensations.

Day 2: Healthy Habits Audit

Task: Take an honest look at your daily habits—nutrition, movement, and sleep.

Evening check-in: Identify which habits support your well-being and which might need improvement.

Day 3: Nourishing Your body

Tasks:

- Aim to incorporate more whole, nutrient-dense foods into your meals.
- Listen to your body's hunger and fullness cues rather than external rules.
- Stay hydrated—drink regularly, not just when you feel thirsty.

Day 4: Movement and Energy

Engage in a form of movement that feels good for your body (e.g., stretching, yoga, dancing, or a walk).

Day 5: Sleep Optimization

- Observe your sleep habits and how they affect your mood, focus, and energy.
- Make small adjustments to improve sleep quality (e.g., reducing screen time before bed, setting a consistent bedtime, creating a relaxing nighttime routine).

Pro tips:

- Try a sleep-tracking app (e.g., Sleep Cycle or Pillow).
- Avoid caffeine or heavy meals close to bedtime.
- Use a calming activity (reading, journaling, or meditation) before sleep.

Day 6: Building Your Stress Management Toolkit

- Identify your top stressors and how they affect your body and mind.

- Practice at least one stress-relief technique today (e.g., breathwork, movement, journaling, or listening to music).

Day 7: Mastering Emotional Regulation

- Learn to name your emotion.
- Try one emotional regulation technique today (e.g., deep breathing, journaling, movement, or grounding exercises).

Week 2: Rewiring Your Thoughts

This week is about challenging limiting beliefs and building confidence.

Day 8: Redefining Challenges

Identify recent challenges. Reflect on how you currently view them —do they feel like obstacles or opportunities to grow?

Day 9: Growth vs. Fixed Mindset

- Reflect on the difference between a growth mindset and a fixed mindset.
- Think back to a moment when you caught yourself thinking with a fixed mindset today. Did you manage to reframe it? How? If not, why?

Day 10: Challenging limiting Beliefs

- Highlight beliefs that hold you back—where did they come from, and are they based on facts or fear?
- Reframe them into empowering beliefs.

Pro tips:

- Use evidence to disprove limiting beliefs; list past achievements or times you proved yourself wrong.

Day 11: Triggering Awareness

- Unpack situations, words, and interactions that make you feel small or unworthy.
- Analyze why these triggers affect you and what underlying beliefs they may be tied to.
- Reframe your responses to these triggers.

Day 12: Exploring Family Mindset

- Recognize the mindset patterns you observed in your family growing up.
- Uncover beliefs about success, failure, and personal growth that may have been passed down.
- Consider which of these beliefs still serve you and which you may need to reframe.

Notes:

- Recognizing generational mindsets allows you to consciously choose your own.
- You can respect your family's values while still redefining what works best for you.

Day 13: Friend Group Analysis

- Think deeply about the people you spend the most time with and how they influence your mindset, habits, and energy.

- Evaluate which friendships uplift and inspire you and which ones may be draining or limiting your growth.

Day 14: Building Your Support System

- Support doesn't have to come from just close friends or family—mentors, online communities, and even books can offer guidance. Go and find them.

Pro tips:

- Be intentional about nurturing relationships that support your growth.
- Quality matters more than quantity—focus on meaningful connections.
- Be open to giving support as well as receiving it; strong relationships are built on mutual care.

Week 3: Unlock Your True Self

You're about raw self-discovery—uncovering who you are beneath expectations, fears, and self-doubt. Each challenge is designed to push your limits, break old patterns, and reveal the real you.

Day 15: Finding Out Who You Are Without Labels

We grow up with labels—some given by others, some we adopt ourselves. But who are you beyond them? Write down a few labels you've been given (smart, shy, responsible, rebellious, etc.). Then, let go of labels that no longer serve you; they don't define your worth.

Day 16: The Non-Negotiables: What Truly Matters to You?

- To build a life you love, you need clarity on your values. Write down:

- o What are my top 5 values? (freedom, creativity, honesty, kindness, etc.)
  - o What things do I refuse to tolerate? (toxic people, unhealthy habits, procrastination, etc.)
  - o How can I match my daily actions with my values?
- Evaluate if your current actions conform to your values and identify any areas that need adjustment.

Day 17: Stepping Into Fear

- Determine one thing that makes you uncomfortable (speaking up in class, trying a new skill, going somewhere alone). DO IT today!
- Notice what felt impossible before you started and how it changed once you faced it.

Pro tips:

- You don't need confidence to begin; courage is built in action.
- Every time you prove fear wrong, you take your power back.

Day 18: Role Models Research

Inspiration is a signal, pointing you toward the version of yourself you're becoming. So, find and list 3-5 role models (both personal and public figures). For each role model, analyze

- what specific qualities draw you to them.
- how they handled setbacks.
- what you can you learn from their journey.
- what qualities you admire most about them, and if they are already within you, waiting to be unlocked.

Day 19: Social Media Audit

- Review the last 10 accounts you interacted with, asking yourself the following questions:
  - How do these make me feel?
  - What messages are they sending me?
  - Do they promote my growth or stir up comparison?
- Unfollow accounts that drain your energy or no longer motivate you. Seek out three new accounts that inspire, educate, and uplift you.

Day 20: Creating Personal Affirmations

Your words shape your reality. Today, recite affirmations that truly resonate with who you are and who you're becoming. Make them personal, powerful, and in the present tense.

- Replace doubt with self-belief: *I am capable.*
- Shift from fear to trust: *I am growing at my own pace.*
- Speak to your worth: *I deserve love and success.*

Pro tips:

- Keep your affirmations specific and meaningful to you.
- Say them out loud with conviction—your voice reinforces their power.
- The more you repeat them, the more they become part of your reality.

Day 21: Turning "Can't" Into "Can"

- Remind yourself that you're not there—yet.
  - List five things you think you can't do.
  - Add **"yet"** to the end of each statement.

- ○ Create action steps to turn each into a possibility.
  - ○ Practice using **"yet"** in conversations and self-talks.
- Consider how "yet" changed the way you see your challenges. Do they feel more possible now?

Week 4: Designing Your Future and Taking Action

Now, it's time to create a roadmap for your future—one that's clear, actionable, and exciting.

Day 22: Defining Your Dream Life

Clarity is the first step to creation. Take time to define your dream life—not based on what others expect, but on what truly fulfill you. Write them down in detail, as if you're already living them.

Pro tips:

- Be specific—details make your vision come alive.
- Focus on feelings, not achievements. Your dream life is about experience, not goals.

Day 23: Mapping Out Your Next Three Years

Set clear, actionable goals for the next three years—goals that relate to the vision you defined yesterday. Break them down into the different areas of your life:

- **Personal growth:** Who do you want to become?
- **Career & finances:** What do you want to achieve?
- **Health & well-being:** How will you take care of yourself?
- **Relationships:** What kind of connections do you want to nurture?

Pro tips:

- Make your goals specific and measurable so progress is clear.
- Write them in present tense, as if they're already happening. Your mind will start believing in them.

Day 24: Skills, Strengths, and What Drives You

Discover the key to your success by recognizing your unique strengths, learned skills, and core motivations. Write them down and connect the dots—how do these elements shape your path? Are you using these strengths and skills to their full potential? What motivation drives you the most?

Day 25: Building Daily Habits for Success

Look at your goals and create a daily habit that will help you reach them. Examples:

- Want to be a writer? Write 200 words a day.
- Want to get fit? Do 10 minutes of movement daily.
- Want to save money? Set aside $1 per day.

Day 26: Overcoming Obstacles Before They Happen

Think ahead—what challenges or setbacks might come up while working toward your goal? For each one, write a solution. Example:

- Challenge: *I might struggle with self-doubt.*
  - Solution: *I will keep a journal of past achievements to remind myself of my progress.*
- Challenge: *I don't have the resources.*
  - Solution: *I will find free learning materials and network with people in my field.*

Day 27: Vision Board Creation

Your dreams deserve a visual space to grow. Create a vision board—digital or physical—that reflects the life you're building. Fill it with images, words, and symbols representing your goals, values, and the energy you want to attract.

Day 28: Manifesting Through Vision

The future you desire starts in your mind. Spend a moment today picturing yourself at your best—your confidence, your energy, your presence. Close your eyes and see the image clearly. Write down what you experience.

Pro tips:

- The brain doesn't distinguish between imagination and reality—visualize with intention.
- Engage all your senses to make the vision feel real.
- Revisit this mental image often—what you see in your mind, you create in your life.

Day 29: Evaluate and Adjust: What's Working?

Look back at your past four weeks and ask yourself these questions:

- *What habit or action had the biggest impact on me?*
- *What isn't working or needs adjustment?*
- *What do I double down on moving forward?*

Day 30: Celebrate Your Wins and Plan What's Next

Even the smallest progress is worth a victory dance! So, why not look back and be amazed by how far you've come by?

- Make a brag list of all the ways you've leveled up, from mindset shifts to new habits.

- Send a thank-you text to those who hyped you up—and maybe bribe them a little to keep doing it.
- Throw a mini party for every tiny win.
- Set new challenges to keep yourself growing.
- Finally, be ridiculously proud of yourself!

Final Challenge Notes:

I came up these four weeks with a lot of thought and care, but I also did so knowing something important: You're the expert of your own life. You know better than anyone what you need right now.

Maybe you're sitting with these thoughts in your mind:

- *I really need to figure out my future first.* (Week 4 is calling your name!).
- *I'm struggling with self-doubt right now.* (Week 2 might be your perfect starting point).
- *I just want to understand myself better.* (Week 1 is there whenever you're ready).
- *I need to break free from what's holding me back.* (Week 3 is waiting for you).

And you know what? You're absolutely right—whatever it is you're thinking. This means you don't have to follow these 30 days in order —let them work for you. Also, Monday isn't the only day for fresh starts; every moment is a new beginning. Your challenge starts whenever YOU say it does!

CONCLUSION

CONGRATULATIONS! UPDATE COMPLETE: Version 2.0 of You has been successfully installed!

So, what's next? If you were expecting a guide, a list of next steps, a structured "do this, then that" kind of thing—sorry, but that's not how it works anymore. You're not the kind of person who needs a script to follow now. You've outgrown that.

You've rewired your neural pathways. Your mind has new connections it didn't have before. Ideas that once seemed impossible now feel within reach. Limits that felt fixed are suddenly flexible. There's no roadmap because you're creating it. No preset rules because you're writing them. You're not waiting for permission. You're not looking for directions. You're the coder now. The architect. The designer of everything that comes next.

However, it's worth noting that right now, two versions of you exist simultaneously.

Version 1.0 is still active—the one with all its familiar patterns, comfortable habits, and predictable responses. It's not gone; it's still running in the background, ready to take control the moment you let it. Version 2.0 is also online—fresh, powerful, and full of potential, but it's not yet your default setting. Not automatically, anyway.

This creates an interesting tension. A battle for bandwidth, if you will.

When you wake up tomorrow, which version will boot up first? When stress hits, which operating system will respond? When opportunities appear, which set of protocols will engage?

The answer isn't simple. It's not about choosing once; it's choosing repeatedly, consciously, deliberately...until the new becomes natural. And if you keep choosing the right way, you won't stop at Version 2.0. You'll build 2.1, 2.2, 2.3—until the upgraded you isn't an option; it's who you are. A growth mindset can take you anywhere you want, so long as you commit to choosing it—again and again.

We learn to evolve, to expand, to break free from the old and step into the new. That's the natural course of growth. But too often, we collect knowledge like souvenirs, admire it for a moment, and then leave it on a shelf while we continue living the same way we always have. Don't let that happen here. Don't read this book just to close it and go back to your old ways.

You've got new tools, new understanding, and new strategies. Basically, you're one step away from world domination, or at least making better life choices. But if all that knowledge just stays trapped in these pages, then all you've done is gather impressive yet useless trivia. Knowledge without action is mental hoarding—cool to have, but ultimately just taking up space. Let's do something with it, shall we?

Use your new mindset daily. Hourly. Or better yet, more often than you check your phone notifications. Your future is calling. It's not patient. It's not going to wait while you get comfortable with the idea of change. It's moving, shifting, unfolding right now—with or without you.

So what's it going to be? Are you going to step up, speak up, and show up in your life in a bigger way? Are you going to let your light shine, your voice be heard, and your power be felt? The choice is yours. Always has been. Always will be. Just be aware that now you've got no excuse. You can't pretend you don't know how. You can't hide behind "I'm not ready" or "I don't know enough." And whatever you decide, decide now. This moment, right here, reading these words—this is your launching point. This is where it starts.

No more waiting.

No more preparing.

No more perfect timing.

Your time is now.

Your move.

And don't forget to share the wealth of your knowledge—because if you can't explain it simply, do you really understand it? Pass it on, help someone else, and in the process, you'll solidify it even more for yourself. It's a double win—they grow, you grow, everyone levels up.

Version 2.0 is live. Hit start and make an impact, Queens!

REFERENCES

Ali, S. A., Begum, T., & Reza, F. (2018). Hormonal influences on cognitive function. *Malaysian Journal of Medical Sciences, 25*(4), 31–41. https://doi.org/10.21315/mjms2018.25.4.3

Bateson, G., Jackson, D. D., Haley, J., & Weakland, J. H. (1956). Toward a theory of schizophrenia. *Behavioral Science, 1*(4), 251–264. https://doi.org/10.1002/bs.3830010402

Beaudoin, K. (2015, March 10). The story of how Lady Gaga became famous will make you like her even more. Mic. Retrieved from https://www.mic.com/articles/112334/the-story-of-how-lady-gaga-became-famous-will-make-you-like-her-even-more

Beck, A. T. (1976). *Cognitive therapy and the emotional disorders.* International Universities Press.

Bian, L., Leslie, S.-J., & Cimpian, A. (2017). Gender stereotypes about intellectual ability emerge early and influence children's interests. *Science, 355*(6323), 389–391. https://doi.org/10.1126/science.aah6524

Blakemore, S. J., & Robbins, T. W. (2012). Decision-making in the adolescent brain. *Nature Neuroscience,* 15(9), 1184-1191. https://doi.org/10.1038/nn.3177

Blakemore, S. J. (2019). Inventing ourselves: The secret life of the teenage brain. PublicAffairs.

Booth, R. (2024, November 29). *'Teenage girls are feeling vulnerable': Fears grow over online beauty filters.* The Guardian. https://www.theguardian.com/media/2024/nov/29/teenage-girls-are-feeling-vulnerable-fears-grow-over-online-beauty-filters

Brambilla, D. J., Matsumoto, A. M., Araujo, A. B., & McKinlay, J. B. (2009). The effect of diurnal variation on clinical measurement of serum testosterone and other sex hormone levels in men. *The Journal of Clinical Endocrinology & Metabolism,* 94(3), 907–913. https://doi.org/10.1210/jc.2008-1902

Brown, B. (2010). The Gifts of Imperfection: Let Go of Who You Think You're Supposed to Be and Embrace Who You Are. Hazelden Publishing.

Burket, J. (n.d.). *22 facts about the brain | World Brain Day.* The Dent Institute. https://www.dentinstitute.com/22-facts-about-the-brain-world-brain-day/

Clance, P. R., & Imes, S. A. (1978). The impostor phenomenon in high achieving women: Dynamics and therapeutic intervention. *Psychotherapy: Theory, Research & Practice,* 15(3), 241–247. https://doi.org/10.1037/h0086006

Damour, L. (2019). *Under pressure: Confronting the epidemic of stress and anxiety in girls.* Ballantine Books.

DePrisco, M. (2022, May 25). *Hiring in a skills-based economy.* Forbes Business Council. https://www.forbes.com/councils/forbesbusinesscouncil/2022/05/25/hiring-in-a-skills-based-economy/

Do you know the factors influencing girls' participation in sports?. (n.d.). Women's Sports Foundation. https://www.womenssportsfoundation.org/do-you-know-the-factors-influencing-girls-participation-in-sports/

Dweck, C. S. (2008). *Brainology.* Independent School. https://www.nais.org/magazine/independent-school/winter-2008/brainology/

Festinger, L. (1957). *A theory of cognitive dissonance.* Stanford University Press.

Fletcher, J. (2019, November 5). *What are the phases of the menstrual cycle?* Medical News Today. https://www.medicalnewstoday.com/articles/326906

14 celebrities who've openly discussed their anxiety struggles. (n.d.). Our Mental Health. https://www.ourmental.health/anxiety/14-celebrities-whove-openly-discussed-their-anxiety-struggles

Frye, H. E., Ko, D., Kotnik, E., & Zelt, N. (2021, October 4). *Policy memo: Motor vehicle crash testing regulations for more inclusive populations.* Washington University in St. Louis. https://sites.wustl.edu/prosper/policy-memo-crash-testing-inclusive/

Gilham, H. (2019, April 24). *All the ways Hera got revenge on Zeus for cheating on her.* Ranker. https://www.ranker.com/list/hera-revenge-on-zeus-cheating/hannah-gilham

Gilovich, T., Medvec, V. H., & Savitsky, K. (2000). The spotlight effect in social judgment: An egocentric bias in estimates of the salience of one's own actions and appearance. *Journal of Personality and Social Psychology, 78*(2), 211-222. https://doi.org/10.1037/0022-3514.78.2.211

Godwin, L. (2025, January 20). *New year, same doubts? Here's how to move forward anyway.* Psychology Today. https://www.psychologytoday.com/us/blog/possibilitizing/202501/new-year-same-doubts-heres-how-to-move-forward-anyway

Goewey, D. J. (2015, August 25). 85 percent of what we worry about never happens. *HuffPost.* https://www.huffpost.com/entry/85-of-what-we-worry-about_b_8028368

Goyanka, R., Gupta, A. K., Bishoyi, D., Nathiya, D., Kaur, P., Shanno, K., Taksande, B. G., Khalid, M., Upaganlawar, A. B., Umekar, M. J., Gulati, M., Sachdeva, M., Behl, T., & Gasmi, A. (2024). Unveiling the Neurotransmitter Symphony: Dynamic Shifts in Neurochemistry Across the Menstrual Cycle. *Reproductive Sciences, 31*(5), 1234–1245. https://doi.org/10.1007/s43032-024-01740-3

Hardesty, L. (2018, February 11). *Study finds gender and skin-type bias in commercial artificial-intelligence systems.* MIT News. https://news.mit.edu/2018/study-finds-gender-skin-type-bias-artificial-intelligence-systems-0212

Hedley, S. (2019, February 25). *Inspiring young girls to pursue STEM careers.* Microsoft. https://www.microsoft.com/en-gb/industry/blog/education/2019/02/25/young-girls-stem-career/

Hendry, E. R. (2013, November 20). *7 epic fails brought to you by the genius mind of Thomas Edison.* Smithsonian Magazine. https://www.smithsonianmag.com/innovation/7-epic-fails-brought-to-you-by-the-genius-mind-of-thomas-edison-180947786/

Kahneman, D. (2011). Thinking, fast and slow. Farrar, Straus and Giroux.

Kapur, M., & Bielaczyc, K. (2012). Designing for productive failure. Journal of the Learning Sciences, 21(1), 45-83. https://doi.org/10.1080/10508406.2011.591717

Kiefer, T. (2018, September 25). What does an effective leader look like? Warwick Business School. https://www.wbs.ac.uk/news/what-does-an-effective-leader-look-like/

Leadem, R. (2017, November 8). *12 leaders, entrepreneurs and celebrities who have struggled with imposter syndrome.* Entrepreneur. https://www.entrepreneur.com/leadership/12-leaders-entrepreneurs-and-celebrities-who-have/304273

Loftus, E. F. (1993). The reality of repressed memories. *American Psychologist, 48*(5), 518–537. https://doi.org/10.1037/0003-066X.48.5.518

Lopez, F. G., & Rice, K. G. (2006). Preliminary development and validation of a measure of relationship authenticity. *Journal of Counseling Psychology, 53*(3), 362–371. https://doi.org/10.1037/0022-0167.53.3.362

What does an effective leader look like? Warwick Business School. https://www.wbs.ac.uk/news/what-does-an-effective-leader-look-like/

Madeleine. (2019, September 13). *What was Zeus and Hera's relationship like?* Theoi. https://www.theoi.com/articles/what-was-zeus-and-heras-relationship-like/

Ma, J. (2017, January 12). 25 famous women on impostor syndrome and self-doubt. The Cut. https://www.thecut.com/article/25-famous-women-on-impostor-syndrome-and-self-doubt.html

Marsh, A. (2024). Fear: An Evolutionary Perspective on Its Biological, Behavioral, and Social Functions. In *The Oxford Handbook of Evolutionary Psychology and Behavioral Endocrinology.* Oxford University Press. https://doi.org/10.1093/oxfordhb/9780197544754.013.25

Millington, A. (2018, July 31). J.K. Rowling's pitch for *Harry Potter* was rejected 12 times — read the now-famous letter here. *Business Insider.* Retrieved from https://www.businessinsider.com/revealed-jk-rowlings-original-pitch-for-harry-potter-2017-10

Murphy, H. (2018, March 17). *Picture a leader. Is she a woman?* The New York Times. https://aom.org/about-aom/aom-news/blog-detail_releases/blog-detail/news/2018/03/17/the-new-york-times-picture-a-leader.-is-she-a-woman

Nelson, L. D., Malkoc, S. A., & Shiv, B. (2018). Emotions, self-protective thinking, and the avoidance of learning opportunities: The emotional cost of failure. *Journal of Behavioral Decision Making, 31*(4), 540–554. https://doi.org/10.1002/bdm.2087

Premack, D., & Woodruff, G. (1978). Does the chimpanzee have a theory of mind? *Behavioral and Brain Sciences, 1*(4), 515-526. https://doi.org/10.1017/S0140525X00076512

Romeo, R. D. (2013). The teenage brain: The stress response and the adolescent brain. *Current Directions in Psychological Science, 22*(2), 140–145. https://doi.org/10.1177/0963721413475445

Schwabish, J. (2024, October 16). *Fact-checking 60,000 thoughts: The mystery behind a misleading statistic.* PolicyViz. https://policyviz.com/2024/10/16/fact-checking-60000-thoughts-the-mystery-behind-a-misleading-statistic/

Sherman, L. E., Payton, A. A., Hernandez, L. M., Greenfield, P. M., & Dapretto, M.

(2016). *The power of the like in adolescence: Effects of peer influence on neural and behavioral responses to social media. Psychological Science, 27*(7), 1027-1035. https://doi.org/10.1177/0956797616645673

SINTEF. (2013, May 22). *Big aata, for better or worse: 90% of world's data generated over last two years.* ScienceDaily. https://www.sciencedaily.com/releases/2013/05/130522085217.htm

Taylor, J. B. (2008). *My stroke of insight: A brain scientist's personal journey.* Viking.

Van Leijenhorst, L., Zanolie, K., Van Meel, C. S., Westenberg, P. M., Rombouts, S. A. R. B., & Crone, E. A. (2010). What motivates the adolescent? Brain regions mediating reward sensitivity across adolescence. *Cerebral Cortex, 20*(1), 61–69. https://doi.org/10.1093/cercor/bhp078

Willman, C. (2008, February 5). Taylor Swift's road to fame: Behind the scenes of the teen sensation's career, from guitar lessons to sold-out shows. *Entertainment Weekly.* Retrieved from https://ew.com/article/2008/02/05/taylor-swifts-road-fame/

Wu, D., Wang, K., Wei, D. *et al.* Perfectionism mediated the relationship between brain structure variation and negative emotion in a nonclinical sample. *Cogn Affect Behav Neurosci* **17**, 211–223 (2017). https://doi.org/10.3758/s13415-016-0474-8

Zauderer, S. (2023, October 5). *79 cell phone/smartphone addiction statistics.* Cross River Therapy. https://www.crossrivertherapy.com/research/cell-phone-addiction-statistics

Zimmerman, M. (1989). The nervous system in the context of information theory. *Journal of Neurophysiology, 42*(1), 116-127.

Made in United States
Orlando, FL
17 June 2025

62191152R00079